2005

Mom

THE **NIGHT**
ᴛᴴᴱ **WHEELS**
ꜰᴱᴸᴸ **OFF**

Stories, Essays, and Other Goofy Stuff

Mike Redmond

To Mark
Best wishes
Mike Redmond
2005

emmis
books

For further information, contact the publisher at

Emmis Books
1700 Madison Road
Cincinnati, OH 45206
www.emmisbooks.com

Library of Congress Cataloging-in-Publication Data

Redmond, Mike, 1954-
 The night the wheels fell off : stories, essays, and other goofy stuff
/ by Mike Redmond.
     p. cm.
  ISBN 1-57860-196-7 (pbk.)
1. Redmond, Mike, 1954- 2. Journalists--United States--Biography. I. Title.
PN4874.R349A3 2005
070.92--dc22

                                        2005002865

Cover designed by Adam Greber
Interior designed by Joni DeLuca
Edited by Jessica Yerega

For Mom and Dad. You made me what I am today.
Or, viewed another way, this is all your fault.

And for Elizabeth.

The Night the Wheels Fell Off

———┃———

Contents

Introduction

The scene: A bookstore in a mall in Central Indiana. The author—a devastatingly handsome man, husky in a grown-up-farm-boy way, with longish brown wavy hair going gray and eyes the color of Darjeeling tea (boy, that's good)— sits on a folding chair behind a draped table at the front of the store, twiddling his thumbs, drinking scorched coffee and occasionally rearranging the stacks of books he is there to autograph for the dozens of readers who, for some reason, have chosen to be somewhere else this afternoon.

He has been parked at the table for forty-five minutes and, so far, has sold two books—one to the bookstore manager and one to the clerk, who come over to the table every ten minutes or so to ask if he needs more coffee (no) and to apologize for the turnout, or lack thereof. "I just can't imagine where everyone is," says the manager. "When that guy from the TV station came to autograph his book, they showed up two hours early and we had a line that stretched clear over to Orange Julius. He brought his dog with him. People sure liked that dog."

"Well, it's a nice dog," says the author, not knowing what else to say.

"Maybe they stayed home because of the weather."

"Yes," says the author. "Only an idiot would get behind the wheel when the sun is shining and the roads are dry."

"I meant they probably had something else to do," the manager explains.

"Oh, I know," says the author. "I checked the TV listings this morning and I knew this was going to be a tough day. Lots of competition for the public's attention. There's a ball game, a race, and PBS is showing a two-hour documentary on snails."

"Really?"

"No."

A woman in a Jeff Gordon sweatshirt approaches the table and picks up one of the books, holding it by the thumb and forefinger, as if it were something green and slimy she just discovered in the back of the refrigerator. The author smiles up at her, expectantly.

"So what's this book about?" she asks.

"Well, it's about family, Indiana kidhood, and other goofy stuff," says the author, quoting the subtitle.

"What does that mean?" She flips through the pages.

"It means it's about my life growing up in Northern Indiana with a bunch of funny people. That's my family on the cover—my grandparents, my mom and her thirteen brothers and sisters and their husbands and wives, and all of us grandkids who had been born to that point. There were a few more to come."

She looks at the cover. "Which one is you?" she asks.

"There. That's me, the kid with the circle around him."

"Doesn't look like you."

"Well, it was a long time ago. I've gained a little weight since then. About two hundred pounds."

No reaction. Nothing. Not even a snicker.

"So this book is about you?" she asks.

"You could say that, although I really think it's about families more than it is about me. It's about the common thread we all…"

"Is it funny?"

"Well, I like to think so. That was my intent when I wrote it, although I also wanted it to have a message about …"

"You think I'd like this book?"

The author bites his tongue—hard, so as to keep him from saying the first thing that pops into his head: "How should I know?" Instead he gives her the pitch: "I am certain of it…" (which, by the way, he is not) "…and besides, my mom really liked it."

No laugh. Not even a smirk.

"Is this what you do? You just write books?" she asks, turning over the book to look at the devastatingly handsome author's picture on the back cover.

"In a manner of speaking. I used to be a newspaper man but I quit to become a freelance…"

"Must be nice. I have to work for my money."

"Well, I've done that, too," he says, keeping to himself the notion that the worst job he ever had, cleaning out hog barns, was a tiptoe through the tulips compared to the amount of manure he is shoveling today.

"How come you just wrote a book about yourself?"

"Well, I couldn't write one about you. I didn't know you well enough."

"Hmm. OK," she says, returning the book to its stack. "I'll think about it."

"I'll be here," says the author, as she wanders off toward Sears.

A half-hour later the woman in the Jeff Gordon sweatshirt walks up to the bookstore again. She brings with her another woman, this one in a Tony Stewart sweatshirt, and it is Tony Stewart Sweatshirt Woman who speaks first.

"I thought that was you!" she says.

"And I thought that was you!" says the author. "Who are you?"

"We're sisters," she says. She turns to Jeff Gordon Sweatshirt Woman. "This is that writer I told you about!" she says.

"The one with the dog?"

"No, the other one. Remember that article I sent you about family reunions and green bean casserole? This is the guy who wrote it." She turns back to the author. "You could have been writing about our family. I loved your columns. I wish you were still writing them. Is this your book?"

"Well, if you mean did I write it, the answer is yes. If you mean do I own it, the answer is no, which makes it available for you to purchase and call your very own." He thinks again of manure shoveling, until the woman picks up three copies and holds them out for him to sign.

"One's for me, one's for my kids, and one's for my Mom," she says.

"God bless you all," says the author. He turns to Jeff Gordon Sweatshirt Woman. "Don't you want one, too?"

"Nah," she says. "I'll just read hers when she's done with it."

As you might have figured out by now, the author is Al Franken. No, it's me. I put in the stuff about being devastatingly handsome to throw you off the trail. And I really did have a day like this, or two, or three, or more, when I was out hustling my first book, *Six of One, Half-Dozen of Another,* copies of which are still available in my hall closet, in a box on the floor of the cab of my pickup, at my mom's house, and at all your finer bookstores and feed mills.

I also had days, many of them in fact, when people lined up to shake my hand (past the Orange Julius stand, and beyond) and told me they liked what

I do and want me to do more of it. Those days made me rethink my plan about taking up the life of a LaGrange County chicken farmer. Those days made me want to write another book. Well, those days, plus the fact that I was under contract.

Six of One was written in anger. I know that may sound silly, given the tone of the book, but it's true. At the time I started writing it, I had just been placed on Double Secret Probation by my employer, and I was mad.

The issue was the content of the newspaper column I had been writing. Under the previous ownership, I had pretty much free reign to write about whatever I wanted to, and it seemed to work fine—I won a few awards, which made the editors happy. Far more important to me, I had a large and loyal audience of readers who liked the way I told stories, especially when I would use my family—my mom, my brother and sisters, my nieces and nephew—to illustrate a larger point about human behavior. That made me happy. Nothing was better than when someone would write to say, "Your family is just like my family." That let me know the point had been made.

Then the newspaper changed hands and the new management team let me know in pretty short order that they did not like, or want, the kind of column I wrote. I kept writing it anyway, which is what led me first to Double Secret Probation, then to *Six Of One*, and then out of the newspaper altogether.

So much for history. Let's just say I'm a much happier person now that I don't dread going into the office anymore, and I hope that happiness will inform the stuff I write these days, including this book. In other words, my life has changed and I have changed, I believe for the better, and it has been interesting to write a book under these conditions.

So here it is—another collection of stories about some people you know—my mom, my brother, my sisters, my cousins—and some people to whom you haven't yet been introduced. It's about me, sort of, but it really isn't.

It might just as well be about you. I suspect you know people like the ones I am going to tell you about. Like me, you may even be related to a few of them (in which case you have whichever you deem appropriate: my heartiest congratulations or my deepest sympathy).

The theme of this book, if there is one (and I'm not sure that's the case), is change. It's about the change that comes to you through the people you meet, the change you bring upon yourself, and the change that just happens to you as a consequence of living. After which, of course, you die.

All my life, I have come to realize, I have been a chameleon, changing to adapt to the circumstances I've found myself in. Sometimes it was following the crowd. Sometimes it was self-preservation. Sometimes it was because I was simply trying out different looks, different attitudes, different ways of life, looking for something that felt like me.

My dentist, Dr. Hilarity, makes fun of it. In the years he has been taking care of my teeth (a process by which my insurance carrier and I have helped him buy several nice homes), he has noted: Preppie Mike, Hippie Mike, Yuppie Mike, Cowboy Mike, Rock and Roll Mike, Biker Mike, Suit and Tie Mike, The Return of Biker Mike, and now, Steady, Solid Middle-Aged Mike with a Touch of Biker Mike Thrown In. And those are just the ones he knows. There were lots of other Mikes before he came into my life.

The thing is, every one of those Mikes was the same guy. They were all me. They were all valid. And they were all part of the process that made me into whatever I am today, and whatever I will be tomorrow.

Well, anyway, here we go with this book, which may or may not say something (I won't know for sure until I'm finished writing) about recognizing the need for change, the need to embrace change, and the need to count your change before you leave the drive-up window. Sorry. I guess I should also point out there will be some goofy stuff in here simply because it's my book and I want it that way.

I hope you like it. What am I saying? I hope you love it and buy multiple copies. A half-dozen per person ought to do it. And be sure to make that freeloading sister of yours buy one, too.

I thank you, and so does my dog.

———— | ————

ONE

Old Enough to Know Better

I am fifty years old now, which just astonishes me. Frankly, I thought turning fifty would be a lot weirder.

I have been on the planet a half-century, longer than I once thought possible and certainly longer than some people might have liked, and I keep waiting for the enormity of those fifty years to fall out of the sky and flatten me. So far, it hasn't happened. Fifty feels a lot like forty-nine, which felt a lot like forty-eight, which felt a lot like forty-seven, and so on. In fact, in many respects I don't feel all that much different than I felt at, say, thirty. This means I am either very young at heart or I have been middle-aged for a long, long time.

It may not be as weird as I thought it would be, but it is not easy being fifty. It isn't. And I'm not just talking about the way my knees pop when I walk up a flight of stairs, or the way it gets harder and harder to lose weight (or even to work up the inclination to lose weight).

Being fifty means I have a half-century's worth of useless information crammed into my head, lying there, gathering dust. Dumb things, like school lunch menus and locker combinations. Camera settings for photos I took thirty-five years ago. Rules of grammar from the third grade that no one seems to remember but me (when two vowels go walking, the first does the talking). Whopping chunks of movie dialogue. Fun Facts to Know and Tell from the backs of cereal boxes ("Kids! Did you know that the Chinese invented gunpowder?" I think that one came from the back of Nabisco Rice Honeys.).

Some of the stuff I could use in a game of Trivial Pursuit, I suppose, if I went in for that game. I don't. And some is stuff which, while trivial, does not seem a likely subject for pursuit—stuff about growing up in rural Indiana in the last half of the twentieth century. Utterly useless. As far as I know, there is no Last Half of the Twentieth Century in Rural Indiana version of Trivial Pursuit.

Like what, you ask? OK, I can remember:

- When you could smoke indoors.
- Black-and-white TV. With three channels.
- Twenty-five-cent movie admission for kids on Saturdays.
- Party lines. And when you dialed the telephone, you actually used a dial.
- My grandmother Redmond cooking on a wood-burning stove and drawing water from a pump at the kitchen sink.
- Outdoor plumbing. Also at Grandma Redmond's house.
- DeSotos.
- Edsels.
- Studebakers.
- Montgomery Ward.
- Dime stores. With candy counters where they made real caramel corn.
- Afternoon newspapers.
- Fifteen-minute newscasts where the weatherman put little stickers on a map, or even better, drew on it with a squeaky magic marker.
- Local kiddie shows, talk shows, and movie shows on TV.
- When every radio station had a news department.
- Five-cent candy bars.
- Ten-cent Hostess Twinkies.
- Twelve-cent comic books.
- Fifteen-cent hamburgers.
- Elsie the Cow, Reddy Kilowatt, Mister Softee, Marky Maypo, the Man from Glad, the Ajax White Knight, Josephine the Plumber, Mr. Whipple, Mrs. Olson, and Aunt Bluebelle.
- Howdy Doody, Jerry Mahoney, and Farfel the dog.
- Duck and cover.
- People getting all worked up over school consolidation. Actually, in some parts of Indiana, they're still not happy about it.
- When telephone numbers began with letters. We lived on the MElrose, FLeetwood, and OLiver exchanges.

See what I mean? Useless. And that's not even the worst of it.

I remember practically every television commercial I have ever seen. I can recite from memory entire stretches of dialogue from *Green Acres* and *Gilligan's Island*. I know the lyrics to about a million pop songs—the right lyrics, too. When "Bad Moon Rising" comes on the radio, you won't catch me singing, "There's a bathroom on the right." Unless, of course, there really is a bathroom on the right—which, when you turn fifty, meaning your bladder has also turned fifty, is the sort of thing you like to know.

I have been told by some people that my memory is phenomenal. They're wrong. It is selective, and it's very good with the things I have selected to remember and very bad with everything else. You will notice what I did not list: algebra, chemistry, history—things I could really use. No, I had to devote those brain cells to knowing Gilligan's first name (Willy) or Mary Ann's hometown (Horner's Corners, Kansas).

And now, because I am fifty, it becomes more and more frustrating. I remember with crystal clarity the words to "Let's Go Fly a Kite" from Walt Disney's *Mary Poppins* ("Let's go fly a kite, up to the highest height, let's go fly a kite and send it soaring, up through the atmosphere, up where the air is clear. Oh, let's go fly a kite!"). I do not, however, remember with any certainty this morning's breakfast, other than it included two blood-pressure pills and a Prozac.

I've been thinking about age since I read a quote from the American Association of Retired Persons about the chronological, but not attitudinal, aging of the Baby Boom generation, my generation.

"Sixty," the quote said, "is the new thirty."

This is troubling. Where does this sort of thinking end? If sixty is the new thirty, does that make thirty the new fifteen? And what of fifteen? Is that the new seven-and-a-half?

Well, no. If anything, fifteen looks an awful lot like thirty these days. Kids mature quickly these days. If you don't believe me just go to a shopping mall, where fifteen-year-olds are known to congregate in great numbers. Sometimes you can't tell them from the thirty-year-olds until they open their mouths and give themselves away by speaking, rather loudly, what teenagers believe to be English.

We're screwy about age in this country, especially we Baby Boomers. I know I am. It seems like we demand that our parents age in a manner we deem graceful ("Mother! You take off that parachute this instant!")...but change the rules when it comes to our own aging. When Dad hit sixty, he was old. When we hit sixty, it's the new thirty.

Actually, my dad was worse than I am when he hit fifty. My sister Amy still gets a twinge of anxiety when she remembers April 28, 1978—Dad's fiftieth birthday. She spent all day baking him a cake and put atop it two big candles, a "5" and a "0." Dad took one look at that cake and stalked out of the kitchen, and he remained in a lousy mood for days.

My dad's middle years were not graceful by any definition of the word. He felt his youth slipping away, and he panicked, and you know what people do when they panic: They do dumb things. In Dad's case that meant girlfriends and heavy drinking and letting what was once a pretty snappy sense of style go by the wayside in favor of jeans, work shirts, tennis shoes, and an ever-present down vest, which was kind of a weird accessory in, say, July.

Dad was flattened by the weight of his fifty years. Maybe that's why I expected it to happen to me. Then again, I have not lived my father's life. For a number of reasons, I think I've been far happier in my fifty years than he was in his, and so his age hit him a lot harder than mine has hit me.

So why was my dad unhappy? Good question. I'd ask him, but he's dead, so I guess I'll just have to try to figure it out for myself.

I think at some level he *decided* to be unhappy. It can work that way, you know. You tell yourself you're going to be miserable and, by God, it usually happens.

My dad was disappointed. His life did not turn out the way he planned. He was a poor kid, a farm kid, who wanted to be a writer. As soon as he could, he lit out from rural Indiana to make his way in the world—at college, in journalism, and then in politics. For a while, he did pretty well for himself, too. But in his middle years it all came undone, and he never really got over it. He found himself back where he started, with not a lot to show for all the time that he had been away. Money? Not a chance. Prestige? Nope. Accomplishment? Not much.

Unless, of course, you count all the people who loved him in spite of his faults. That is a great accomplishment in my book. It's the only accomplishment that matters, and I wish Dad could have seen it that way.

My dad was disappointed that he never wrote any of the books he promised himself he would write. Mostly he was just disappointed in himself, although I doubt you could have gotten him to admit that. When it came down to the question of taking responsibility for his failings or blaming them on circumstances, Dad tended to blame circumstances. I guess most humans do, and that's why the people who really *do* stand up and say, "Nope, sorry, that was my fault," are so scarce.

Well, anyway, Dad hit fifty in the middle of all that mess. No wonder Amy's cake set him off. He assigned way more importance to a number than it deserved.

Dad was all whacked out about being middle-aged. Maybe it's because he didn't have this to help—Mike's Handy Guide to Identifying the Middle Age Danger Signals:

- You yell at the kids to turn down the stereo.
- The kids yell at you to turn down the news.
- Out: bourbon, scotch, and beer. In: Zocor, Rogaine, and Viagra.
- You buy jeans for how they fit, not how they look.
- All your shoes are slip-ons.
- You remember every word of a Frosted Flakes commercial from forty years ago, but under threat of torture you would not be able to name what you had for dinner two nights ago.
- There is not a single professional athlete your age. Not even a golfer or bowler.
- You watch the Weather Channel. Eight, ten hours at a time.
- You used to go to the doctor, singular. Now you have doctors.
- And half of those doctors are younger than you.
- Your kid has to bail you out when you "accidentally" visit hotbustycheerleaderswholoveoldermen.com and the computer locks up.
- You open the engine compartment of your car and recognize not one single component.
- When you have a problem with a tooth, the dentist sends them out to be fixed.
- Trying to read with your first pair of trifocals makes you throw up.

- You can't remember the last time you saw a movie about people your own age.
- Everything you eat gives you gas.
- You find yourself home on a Saturday evening watching a rerun of *The Lawrence Welk Show* on PBS … and enjoying it.
- You know how to fix things that are no longer manufactured.
- You catch an old episode of *I Love Lucy*, and you see Fred Mertz walking around in pants that belt somewhere around his armpits, and you think to yourself, "You know, that looks kind of comfortable."
- When faced with a choice between sex and Key lime pie, you actually have to think it over.

I am not telling which ones apply to me. I will say I have never been overly fond of Key lime pie. Apple, however, is a different story.

Here's the way I wish it were: However many years ago you were born, that's how old your body is, and it's really no big deal until it gets up into the impressive numbers. Like, oh, 127. What you do with that body, however old, is up to you. Well, you and your physician if you want to throw it out of airplanes.

Just be whatever age you are, do the best you can with it, and have as much fun as possible, however you want. I find myself drawn to Mae West's adage: "Age doesn't matter, unless you're cheese." Of course, Mae turned into a pretty moldy piece of Camembert toward the end, but still I can relate to what she said. By her measure I am a nice chunk of aged cheddar, sharp on the tongue and maybe a little dried out around the edges, but mellow and smooth beneath the bite.

In other words, my birth certificate says I am fifty. Or you could say I am the new twenty-five. In Mae West years, however, I have reached the age where I go perfectly with a warm piece of apple pie. And a Prozac.

Important Lessons

I just got off the phone with a furnace repairman. A little while ago I noticed the smell of something burning here in my office. I had rather hoped it was my computer, which is four years old and therefore about seventeen generations out of date, so I could order up one of those fancy-shmancy new muscle machines with gobs of storage and power, all the better for when I go Web surfing and accidentally land on that Naughty Brunette Housewives site. I mean, on Low-Cal Recipes for Modern American Living.

Anyway, it turned out not to be my computer after all, but the furnace, which had abdicated its job of pumping nice, clean heat through the house and was instead filling it with the aroma of smoldering plastic. As odors go, it was noxious, but at the same time nostalgic. It smelled exactly like when my cousin Grant and I strapped one of my brother's G.I. Joes to a Roman candle in what we shall call a childhood experiment in low-altitude air travel. However, Joe was too heavy for the rocket, and instead of zooming into the sky, he just sort of stood there on the ground surrounded by smoke and flames, staring stoically ahead, like the good soldier that he was. Then he fell over. The rocket continued to spark and hiss, and then exploded. When the smoke cleared, we found that instead of Rocket Man, G.I. Joe had become Melted Head Man.

So anyway, I call the furnace man and tell him that my three-year-old Blast-O-Matic 9000 smells like someone is using it to roast G.I. Joes.

"Huh?" he says.

"Burning plastic. My furnace smells like burning plastic."

"Oh, OK. We can have a repair truck there this afternoon," says the furnace man. "Is someone going to be at the house?"

"Yes, I'm here all day, every day."

"Retired, huh?"

Well, didn't that just frost my pumpkin.

I am not retired. True, I left the newspaper business in 2003 after twenty-eight good years and two rotten ones. But I am not retired. I am a writer. There's a difference. For one thing, all the retired guys I know work a lot harder than I do. Take a look around your neighborhood for a place with a perfect lawn, a spotless car, and a perfectly arranged workshop with all the tools hanging in their assigned places on a pegboard. That's the home of a guy who retired from a forty-hour-a-week job to take care of all those things at home. Which requires about sixty hours a week.

Me, I spend my days parked in front of an aging computer making fun of things and trying to figure out ways to turn this enterprise into cash. This is not all that different from the way my life used to be when I worked at a newspaper, except there they came around once a week to give me money whether I needed it or not. OK, I always needed it.

I alluded to my departure from the newspaper business in the Introduction which you did not read, Introductions being the part of the book everybody skips, usually with good reason. Too often they contain a whole bunch of thank-yous to people who mean absolutely nothing to the reader: "Thank you, Biff, for being there … thank you, Lorinda, for standing with me in my hour of need … thank you, Zelda and Agamemnon, for being there and standing with me."

Well, phooey. I don't know any Biffs or Lorindas or Zeldas or Agamemnons. OK, there was one Zelda, but that was a long time ago and I don't think she'd remember me. Besides, she was a springer spaniel.

Basically, as I mentioned in the introduction, when I left the newspaper business, I was presented with a good time to take stock of myself—who am I, where am I, how did I get here, what have I learned, and where am I going? I've been at it for about a year now and can confidently report that I am no closer to the answers than when I started.

One thing that is different these days is that I have to scramble to make a living. This is new for me. I entered the workforce for good at age seventeen, and since then I have never, for more than a couple of weeks anyway, been without a place to go to work.

One of the ways I make that living now is by public speaking. It's a good deal. Agents find gatherings of people who eat large amounts of institutional food, and somehow convince the organizers that I would be just the perfect addition to the dessert course. I show up, make a few smart-aleck remarks, and they give me money. It's quite a racket, when you think about it.

My training for this line of work actually goes back to elementary school. In fifth grade, I was yanked out of my regular school, a place I liked exceedingly well, and stuck into a "special school for gifted children," which I detested. This was mostly because I had been removed from a classroom in which the ratio of fun people to twerps was about twenty to one, and placed in an environment where the twerps were the overwhelming majority—again, by about twenty to one.

(Twerp, for the purposes of this discussion, refers to people who do extra-credit projects, who always know the answer no matter what the subject, and who do not hesitate to remind the teacher that she has forgotten to assign homework for the weekend. Twerps are the people who, in a normal school, would be ambushed in an alley on the way home from school and beaten to within an inch of their lives every single day. Imagine being in an entire classroom of people like this. I still have bad dreams about it.)

Anyway, one of the features of this special school was the Daily Talk. Every day, a different member of the class would have to give a presentation, complete with visual aids and an outline, on a subject of his or her choosing. The class would then vote on the quality of the presentation, giving us not only a taste of public speaking, but our first experience with office politics as well. Popular kids were voted "outstanding" and "excellent," no matter how dull their talks. The rest of us struggled to get "very good" and "good" on our talks.

I well remember the day our new fifth grade teacher told us about the Daily Talk program. I remember it because she chose me to give the first one.

I had six weeks to work on the talk. Naturally, I waited until the sixth day of the fifth week to begin. My subject, I had decided, would be volcanoes.

Why? I have no idea. I had no special interest in volcanoes. I honestly think it was just the first subject to pop into my head. It could have just as well been "baseball" or "spit" or "megaphones," but my head was tuned to the Volcano Channel that day. It never occurred to me that my classmates might not care to hear about volcanoes, whereas they might very well pay rapt attention to a presentation on spit. I was going the volcano route. My mind was made up.

At about 6 P.M. the night before I was to give the talk, I dragged out the "V" volume of the encyclopedia and began copying everything it said about volcanoes and especially about the city of Pompeii, which fascinated me because of the way the bodies of its victims had left molds, if you will, in the hardened volcanic ash. I was right in the middle of my monster movie phase, you see, and the idea of people being buried under volcanic ash really appealed to me, as long as it happened a long time ago and not in my neighborhood.

"What are you working on?" asked my father.

"A report about Pompee-eee," I said.

"Pom-PAY," said Dad.

"Pom-PAY. Not Pompee-eee?"

"No. And what have you learned about Pompeii?" asked Dad.

"It got buried by Mount Ve-su-VEE-us."

"Read some more."

I hit the books for a solid twenty minutes more. That took care of the report.

For visual aids, I drew a couple of pictures of erupting volcanoes, heavy on the smoke and lava and screaming victims. I clipped a few pictures of Mount Vesuvius and Pom-PAY from a National Geographic I found in one of the stacks in the basement. And then I decided I should also make a model of a volcano, which led to another exchange with my father:

Mike: "Hey, Dad, where do we keep the gunpowder?"

Well, actually, it wasn't an exchange because he didn't say anything. Not with words. His facial expression clearly indicated, however, that we did not have any gunpowder, and if we did, I would be the last person he would tell. A lot of good it did knowing that the Chinese invented the stuff if my own father didn't even keep any around for when a guy needed it.

So my plans for a spectacular exploding volcano as a visual aid went by the wayside, and instead I slammed together a cone of green Play-Doh with red Play-Doh lava running down the sides, with a puff of cotton smoke coming out of the top. Well, that's what I was shooting for, anyway. It suffered a little in transit to school the next day. My volcano ended up looking like something I scraped off the sidewalk at the bus stop.

As class began I assembled my visual aids, gathered up my note cards, and …oh, forget it. You and I both know what happened: I thought I could wing it and I tanked the speech. I was unprepared, and I did a sloppy job. Which, of course, would have been a valuable lesson, had I bothered to take note of it. Not me. Nope. No siree.

No, the lesson I took was that from now on, whenever I had to make a talk, I would wing it on a subject with which I was familiar. It is a rule I follow to this day, which is why most of my speeches end up being about whatever stupid things I've done lately.

The Daily Talk was pretty much it for me and public speaking until I got to high school, where I joined the speech team in my junior year for the same reason any boy joins the speech team: A girl. I had a major heater for a classmate who shall remain nameless but whose initials were D.E.B.B.I.E. B.A.N.A.S.I.A.K. She joined the speech team, so I joined the speech team. Not that I ever told her about the heater. She was going steady with my good friend Mel Sautter, and that made her off-limits. Besides, I was the admire-from-afar type anyway, or as at least from as afar as you could get in a small school like Lakeland.

You had to choose an area of speech competition. I considered several— Humorous Interpretation, Oratorical Interpretation, Original Oratory, Original Interpretation of Oratorical Humor, and of course, Babbling About Subjects Nobody Except You Finds Interesting, Such As Volcanoes. They looked like big pains in the butt, which is what led me to compete in Radio Broadcasting. It seemed like the least amount of work.

Here's the setup: Each speech meet was divided into four rounds, and the first two were easy. They gave you things to read—music introductions and commercials. You read them into a microphone while the judges listened through speakers in another room. Cake.

The third round was a newscast. You were given a pile of wire service copy and had a short time to assemble it into a two-minute newscast. Not exactly cake, but it wasn't hard labor, either.

The final round was the tough one. It was on-the-spot broadcasting. You'd get a slip of paper with a headline on it—*Five injured in brawl over Monopoly game at family reunion*, let's say—and you would have to improvise a ninety-second report from the scene. This was difficult, and especially so for me. I usually ran out of things to say at about the twenty-second mark.

My buddy Mike Pipher and I competed together in broadcasting, and Mike was good at it. He had a warm baritone radio voice, an easy delivery, and a genuine interest in broadcasting. I, on the other hand, was more or less along for the ride. I had a tenor voice that became more tenor with nerves, and a rather choppy way of reading aloud—my attempt to mimic the cadences of David Brinkley. Actually, it made me sound like someone who was not entirely familiar with English, and probably not all that fluent in his native language, either. And as far as my interests were concerned, we've already covered that: D.E.B.B.I.E. B.A.N.A.S.I.A.K.

So Mike coasted along collecting blue ribbons at speech meets, and I brought up the rear. I usually placed about fifth, down in green ribbon territory. It went like this for two years, right up through the state speech tournament our senior year. Mike got the blue ribbons in sectionals and regionals; I barely stayed alive, scraping into the next rounds just under the wire with my greenies.

And so off we went to the state speech contest in Peru, Indiana, the city of my birth, with Blue Ribbon Mike Pipher leading the charge. Anyone could see that Mike was going to do very well at the state contest and that I would be lucky to last until lunchtime. Heck, I would have been the first person to say so. In fact, I think I was.

That was OK. The contest started so early in the morning that the school agreed to put us up in a hotel the night before it. To get to go out of town and stay in a hotel on the school's dime? As far as I was concerned, I was a winner already.

We got to Peru the night before the contest—Mike, myself, Victor Bruni (who competed in Impromptu, one of the really difficult categories), and Jim Garver, who had qualified as an alternate. We settled into our rooms—Mike and I in one, Victor and Jim in another. And this is where we go through the looking glass.

Mike and I had made friends with some cadets on Howe Military School's speech team, and by prior arrangement they came to our room for a few hands of poker. With them, they brought two six-packs of Carling Black Label beer.

Well, folks, the poker gods were rooting for Lakeland High School that night. Mike and I were on fire. Straights, flushes, full houses flew out of the deck and into our waiting fingers. What hands Mike didn't win, I did. Pretty soon, the cadets were out of money and out of beer. We had won it all. And then we drank it. The beer, not the money.

I noticed something out of the ordinary upon waking up the next morning. Because of the combination of a late night and a copious quantity of beer, my voice was now somewhere down under the carpet. A few hours earlier, I had been a reedy tenor; now, thanks to exhaustion and the brewing arts, I could sing bass for the Jordanaires. I sounded like ... a *radio* guy. One of those lugubrious small-town radio guys who reads the funeral notices and furniture commercials on the local FM station, maybe, but a radio guy just the same.

We went off to the competition and for the first three rounds, Mike seemed relaxed and confident. He looked to be on track to win a ribbon, just as expected. Seeing as how I didn't really feel like I belonged there anyway, I just sort of breezed through my performances, investing in them the sort of effort and attention to detail usually reserved for, oh, scratching your ear. I did get a lucky break when the music copy I was given to read included the name Modest Mussorgsky. I had studied Russian briefly, you see, and even though I couldn't remember but a few scattered phrases (*"Excuse me. Do you have any toilet paper?"*), I could pronounce Russian names. It also helped that I knew Mussorgsky's music. But it didn't really make a lot of difference to me. Like I said, I was just along for the ride.

Mike and I both made it to the final round, the on-the-spot broadcast. Mike went first, his usual unflappable self. When he came out of the booth, he said he thought he did all right, which, you may take it from me, meant he nailed it.

A short while later, it was my turn. I sat down behind the microphone and picked up the piece of paper that lay facedown on the desk. This would be my subject, the thing I would have to talk about, with no preparation, for the next ninety seconds. It was a plane crash on the runway at the airport in Las Vegas.

I got the signal and began talking:

"This is Jarvis Barnstead coming to you live from the tarmac of Las Vegas International Airport where a passenger plane bound for Saskatchewan has crashed upon takeoff, sending a column of smoke and fire into the air and ..." Blah, blah, blah. I did what I always did: I babbled. I babbled about the passengers and the emergency crews and the flames and the smoke and the wreckage and the heat and the poisonous gas. I babbled until I had absolutely nothing more to say, not an idea left in my head, and looked at my watch.

I still had forty-five seconds to fill. This would have been a problem if I had taken the competition seriously. Since I didn't, however, I went with the first ridiculous idea that popped into my head. I said:

"That's all I can see from here. For more details, let's go to my colleague, Robert Ringworm, on the other side of the airplane."

And then I started babbling again—as another person. Same airplane, same smoke and fire, same victims, same emergency crew, but in another voice, from the other side of the airplane: "Thank you, Jarvis. From here I can see the pilot waving frantically to the ground crew ..."

What the hell. I had nothing to lose. I was just playing around at that point, happy to be there, just glad to be a part of it, honored to be chosen, all that Oscar-nominee stuff. Then I went back out to rejoin my friends and await the results.

An hour ticked by and the announcement went through the building: Final results were being posted outside the auditorium. I sauntered down the hall to see just how badly I had done and got the shock of my life.

I won.

Jarvis and Robert and I had placed first in radio broadcasting.

Staying up late the night before playing cards and drinking beer, going to a speech meet with a hangover, goofing off, doing whatever popped into my head, pretending to be two different people, making things up, *babbling*, I won the state championship.

Not only that, but I had placed first in every round of competition.

I honestly thought there had been a mistake. I wasn't *supposed* to win. I was the guy who was along for the ride. All my life I had been told that success came only through hard work and elbow grease. It just didn't make sense that I could win a state championship by being a smart aleck, but I did.

There were lessons in this. As usual, I missed them. All I could see was that suddenly it seemed possible indeed to be rewarded for goofing off, and I clung fast to this belief far longer than I should have. In fact, I think I finally let go of it for good about two weeks ago.

What I should have taken from it, of course, is that you do your best work when you are relaxed—which, I have come to understand, is not the same thing as hungover—and that the best time to take chances is when you have nothing to lose. But I wasn't clever enough to figure that out right then. For years, the only thing I took from it was a trophy, which has long since been misplaced. I think it's somewhere in the attic over the garage, along with the Christmas decorations, old guitars, and busted vacuum cleaners. Either that or I left it at Mom's, which means it's going to come back to me one of these days in a box marked "Mike Junk" with a note saying "I thought you moved out thirty years ago. Why didn't you take this crap with you?" Mom's sentimental like that.

I did find these lessons making sense to me, however, when I embarked on my new career as a public speaker (as opposed, I guess, to a private one). I try to present a relaxed, confident Mike to the audiences that hire me, and I try to give them the best I can, whether it's a corporate gig or a church social. The corporate gigs, of course, are the more lucrative of the two, but the church social gigs always have better food, especially the desserts. There's a church in Clinton County, Indiana, where the ladies make a chocolate fudge bar that is so sweet, so rich, and so decadent it can wipe out thirty years' worth of good dental hygiene with one bite. It's almost sinful, that's how good it is. Which raises an interesting theological question: Why is all this sinfully good food served in church basements?

Most of the time, I have a lot of fun at these things. I tell a few stories, take a few questions, try to impart a message or two if that's what the client wants, and sell a few books. I always make a lot of new friends and we always have a pretty good time. In fact, I can only think of one time when I really, really bombed. We're talking giant stinkburger, folks. Although I don't think it was all my fault.

Indianapolis was host city to a convention of archery retailers, and I was booked to speak at a customer appreciation party for a company that makes arrows. "We want something funny, something lighthearted, something our customers can relate to," the company spokeslady told me. Cool. Funny I can do. Lighthearted I can do. And as far as relating to the customers, heck, I was an archer myself once, and so were a bunch of my cousins. Archery stories? Piece of cake.

Like the fact that my mother didn't think I was responsible enough for a shotgun, which I wanted, and instead got me a hunting bow. Excuse me? I can't have a shotgun but I can have this thing that sends deadly pointed projectiles zooming off in a variety of directions, only occasionally including the direction I actually intended? Good thinkin', Mom.

Or the time we didn't have any bottle rockets, so my cousin John tied a bunch of sparklers to an arrow, lit them up, and sent them streaking into the night sky. It was a great effect until they burned out and we didn't have any idea where the arrow was coming down. You never saw kids run into the garage so fast in your life.

Or the time my cousin Nate was just dinking around with a bow and pulled off the shot of a lifetime by shish kebabbing a gopher that happened to be running across his path.

So off I went to the event, in a meeting room at a hotel, and as soon as I got there I knew I was in trouble.

For starters, I was the only guy wearing a necktie. From what I could see, I may have been the only person to even *own* a necktie. Everyone else was in hunting camoflage, and wearing their hats indoors. They all looked like they were going to go whack Bambi as soon as they finished their beers. This was not a good sign. And when I tried to explain my attire by opening with, "Well, I see *someone* didn't get the memo concerning the dress code," nobody cracked a smile.

The meeting room was set up with a bar at one end, a buffet at the other, with the stage in the middle. There were cocktail-lounge tables arranged around the room and next to the stage, and two large serving tables were stacked high with my book, *Six of One, Half-Dozen of Another.*

The president of the company introduced me. I clambered up onto the stage, took the microphone out of the stand, and wheeled into my routine.

And nobody was looking at me.

All around the room, the conventioneers were engaged in conversation, getting food, standing in line for drinks. All my stories, all my material was just so much background noise. I knew within ten seconds that I was going to bomb. Which left me twenty-nine minutes, fifty seconds in which to do it.

I ran through my archery stories. I even went so far as to act them out as I did it, thinking that if they saw some movement on the stage, they might at least glance that way. No dice. They sat there, heads down, drinking their beers and eating their pasta, telling their own jokes to each other.

I decided to ratchet it up and started drawing more stories out of my memory banks, stories that had laid 'em in the aisles all over Indiana, proven bits about growing up on a farm in LaGrange County, about my misadventures with my brother, about my pal Raymond Fenzel.

Nothing. Not so much as a chuckle.

Finally, after twenty minutes, I called it quits. Not that anyone noticed.

The spokeslady for the archery company came up to me. She was apologetic. "I guess it just wasn't a very good mix," she said.

Gee, I thought, *what was your first clue? Could it be the fact that they were more interested in dried-out fettuccine Alfredo than the speaker?*

"It's not your fault," she added. "I was talking to a couple of them and when they heard you were a writer, they said that meant you had gone to college and you'd probably use words they didn't understand."

At that moment, I was thinking some words I know they would have understood.

"Maybe they were a little intimidated," she added. "They're all from small towns, they're outdoors types, and for some of these folks, this is probably the nicest party they've ever been to."

"Oh, well," I said. "It happens sometimes. Sometimes you connect with an audience and other times it just doesn't happen. They're all from out of town and maybe that had something to do with it. Yeah, that could be it."

To tell the truth, I was humiliated. Maybe if the bar had been closed, maybe if the food line had been closed, I might have had a chance. Maybe not. I don't know. The fact remained that I had flopped, and I even thought, for a moment, about refusing their check.

Then I came to my senses.

Which, of course, is the lesson. Always take the check. Always. It isn't a reflection of your worth. It is payment for your work.

Besides, you never know when your furnace is going to explode.

THREE

Turn Your Head and Laugh

For the last twenty years or so, my health—such as it is—has been entrusted to Dr. Robert W. Mouser of Indianapolis. This is the first time I have referred to him in print by his real name. Usually I call him Dr. Shecky, the world's funniest (he thinks) family physician.

Shecky, of course, refers to Shecky Greene, the alleged comedian. I gave Dr. Mouser the name because he carries with him—in addition to a prescription pad, a stethoscope, and one of the finest minds I have ever encountered—a seemingly inexhaustible supply of cornball jokes.

Example:

"Mike, I have bad news. You've got Dunlop's disease. You're belly's done lopped over your belt."

And:

"The three signs of aging are losing your memory, and I can't remember the other two."

And:

"What's that in your pocket? A pack of Camels? Haven't you heard? Nine out of ten doctors who've tried Camels prefer women."

And:

Well, I can't repeat the fourth one. It's dirty. But you may rest assured that it's also cornball.

Shecky is a short, roundish man with a bald head and thick glasses. He resembles a Muppet, and not just any Muppet. Shecky is a ringer for Dr. Bunsen Honeydew, who was also roundish with a bald head and thick glasses. Remember him from *The Muppet Show*? He was the one who gave the reports from Muppet Labs, where something always blew up in the face of his assistant, Beaker. Well, if you've seen Dr. Bunsen Honeydew, you've seen Shecky. The difference, of course, is that Dr. Bunsen Honeydew goes around all day with a human arm sticking into his posterior, whereas Shecky does not, although he does have a little experience with posterior regions. More about that in a bit.

Shecky used to carry a large fake pill in the pocket of his coat —a paper-weight, I am guessing, given to him by one of the pharmaceutical salesmen who now litter his office with pamphlets and ballpoint pens. The pill was cooler. Imagine taking a two-inch slice out of the center of a softball. That was the size of Shecky's clown pill.

After examinations, he used to produce the pill and tell children to take it with a glass of water. Big laugh. He also pulled the same joke on adults, with one change: He told them it was a suppository. Bigger laugh. His laugh, I mean. Some of those kids thought he meant it. So did some of the adults.

I started seeing Shecky when I first moved to Indianapolis. I had the epizootic, the name my grandma gave the malady that leaves you with a runny nose, a hacking cough, violent sneezing, watery eyes, and mild fever. You begin to hear noises from your chest that sound like someone stepped on an accordion. And you have the general feeling that everything would be all right if someone would just drag you out behind the barn and shoot you.

I needed a doctor, and Shecky was first on the list provided to me by the find-a-doc service in the yellow pages. Half-delirious with fever, oxygen-deprived from my stuffed nasal cavities, I went to his office. He looked into my nose, made a booger joke, listened to my chest, made the Dunlop's disease joke for the first of what would be several hundred times, gave me a general going-over, made the suppository joke, wrote a prescription, and sent me on my way. In a few days I was cured and really didn't give Shecky a whole lot of thought until the next year, when I caught the epizootic again.

I didn't make Shecky my doctor for real until a couple of years after that, during my wild bachelor days, when my life was dedicated to the pursuit of ... well, you know what wild bachelors pursue. This pursuit led one day to the arrival in my mailbox of a postcard from a particular public medical institution that specializes in the treatment of maladies of an intimate sort contracted by the pursuit of ... well, you get the picture. Now, this institution is known for its tenacity in tracking down cases like this, which is good. When an agency is charged with the responsibility of keeping certain maladies from becoming epidemic, you want it staffed by people who do not take no for an answer.

But—and this is the God's honest truth, in case my mom is reading—the postcard was in error. Evidently I popped up on someone's list of possible infectees. Why? I have a theory. This was once considered a good way to get even with someone with whom you were angry, and I think that's what happened here. All I know for sure is that I know I didn't have any of Those Diseases because I had not done anything by which one can get Those Diseases. Hey, I only said I was engaged in the wild bachelor's pursuit. I did not say I was successful.

Well, anyway, the bulldogs were after me, insisting that I come down to the clinic and get the old once-over.

I decided I would be more comfortable to have my physician do the once over, thank you very much, and told them so. Fine, they said, but we'll need his name and number so we can call him with all the pertinent information, and then we're going to bug you to make sure you do, in fact, go. I gave them Shecky's name and number.

Now, as it turns out, I was in the middle of my annual bout with the epizootic. Some people set their years by the calendar; I set mine by my nasal passages and bronchial tubes. So I called Shecky and said I needed an appointment to take care of my stuffy nose, my nagging cough, my high-velocity sneezing, and some other business, also.

While this was going on the clinic was following up as well, calling Shecky to let him know what that other business might be. I know this because of what happened when I went to the doctor's office that afternoon. I was sitting in the examining room when Shecky opened the door, glanced at the chart, fixed me with a look, and said:

"Well, I guess I don't have to ask what you've been up to lately."

That was it. I knew I had found my doctor.

And thus it has been ever since. In the last twenty years, I have followed Shecky through four offices. I have driven to those four offices from six different residences and paid for his services with at least that many different insurance carriers, but I've never once considered going to any other physician.

One thing I especially like about Shecky is that he is older than me. He's about seventy, give or a take a year. The older I get, the more that means to me. I've been to doctors who are younger and—guys, you'll understand this—it is just plain unsettling to have another guy, half your age, telling you to turn your head and cough. Don't even start with me on someone half your age and the opposite sex.

Once when I was in Hawaii, I became deathly ill and had to be treated by a hotel doctor who seemed to be all of about fourteen. He scolded me for not seeking medical attention sooner. I told him to knock it off and write a prescription or I'd let the air out of the tires of his bicycle. I refuse to be scolded by someone who isn't old enough to shave.

Shecky was the doctor who ushered me into middle age with The Examination Every Man Over Forty Must Have and Cannot Stand. If you do not understand what I mean, you are either a woman, in which case you can ask a man what I mean, or you are a man under forty, in which case you have an unpleasant surprise in your future.

I'm not sure the fact that he was older made this procedure better, necessarily, but I *do* know I wouldn't have wanted it done by Doogie Howser. If someone has to make me into a hand puppet, let it be Shecky.

I learned a lot that day. I learned that men really are the incredible weenies women say we are. If The Examination Every Man Over Forty Must Have and Cannot Stand is any indication of what women have to go through—and I have it on good authority (women) that it is but a tiny *fraction* of the indignities they must endure in the name of good health—they would have to sedate me to get me to the gynecologist.

I also learned that I am in good shape down there, if that matters.

And when Dr. Shecky snapped on his rubber glove and told me to bend over and grab something sturdy, and then did what he had to do in The Examination Every Man Over Forty Must Have and Cannot Stand, I learned that in times of stress, I am strong enough to pick up an examining table.

I like Shecky because he is a well-rounded person. He is an Air Force veteran, during which time he did something for the government so secret that he's not supposed to talk about it. He is a well-known and highly regarded collector of art. When he was twelve, he and a friend wrote a book about astronomy. He was in on the development of Gatorade. You can learn a lot from him.

And how do I know all this? Because when I go to see Shecky, we talk.

Shecky still believes that the biggest, most important part of a medical examination is the conversation between doctor and patient. Having been to assembly-line medical practices in the days Before Shecky (B.S.), I still can't quite believe it when he acts like he has all the time in the world to talk with me.

This is what led him, at an age when most people retire, to leave a hospital-run medical group, one of those things that is a Health Maintenance Organization mostly as it applies its own financial health, and start over as an independent. The hospital's bean counters require their physicians to run something like twelve patients an hour through their offices, and Shecky told them to take their beans and put them … well, let's just say if they did what he said and were men, the bean counters would certainly have some explaining to do next time they had The Examination.

Another reason I like Shecky is that he tells good stories, the kind you can only get when you've been doing something for about fifty years, as he has.

Shecky was once the youngest physician in the city. Remember that Doogie Howser guy I told you about in Hawaii? Shecky, once upon a time, was the Indianapolis version—he was out of high school and blazed through college and was Dr. Mouser before he was twenty years old. I wonder if some cranky middle-aged patient once threatened to let the air out of *his* bicycle tires. If I know Shecky, he would have just laughed and given him a jab with a tongue depressor.

Because he was young and unmarried, his medical colleagues recommended him for the job of house physician at the Fox Theater, Indianapolis's fabled burlesque house. Now, when he told me this, it got my attention right away, seeing as how I am such a big fan of the performing arts.

He was called to the theater one night to see to the medical needs of a performer by the name of Countess Barassa, who had come down with an awful case of walking pneumonia, probably as a result of going out without her hat on. Or much else.

The Countess was in awful shape when Shecky walked in, black bag in hand. She needed a large dose of penicillin delivered in the most efficient way, via hypodermic needle. The usual place for delivery of such a dose is in what medical science refers to as the buttockular region, and this is where Shecky planned to impale the Countess with a couple million units of Better Living Through Pharmaceuticals.

"Oh, no you don't," she told him. "If it leaves a bruise, I won't be able to work."

Shecky, ever mindful of the need of his patients to earn a living, asked where he might be able to give her the shot, seeing as how just about any place he might choose would likely be on display at some time or another in the Countess's act.

She pointed, and gave her a gigantic shot of penicillin … in the armpit.

It hurts just to think about it.

Shecky told me this story just as I was going to get a gigantic shot of something. I don't remember what, only that it wasn't penicillin. And then he left the room and made his nurse do the dirty work. I guess I didn't hold the same allure as the Countess.

I got the shot where you're supposed to. Not the armpit. The other end. And I counted myself lucky it wasn't The Examination. As I left, limping slightly, I ran into Shecky in the hallway.

"Thanks for coming in," he said. "I feel so much better now." That's his standard exit line. It never fails to get a laugh. His. Like I said, he's the world's funniest (he thinks) family physician. The thing is, he's right.

FOUR

The Further Adventures of Mike and P.D.

Throughout my life, I have always known that there was one person I could trust, one person I could count on when the chips were down, one person to whom I could confide my secrets and confess my fears. I always knew this person would be there for me, listening without judging, and would support me faithfully in anything I did. But enough about my therapist.

I also have a brother, P.D., whom I trust, up to a point. By that I mean I put my complete faith and confidence in my brother, as I know he does in me, on things like ... oh, life. But on the really *important* stuff, such as, say, collecting toy farm tractors, I wouldn't trust him as far as I could throw him, and neither would he trust me.

You see, being brothers, as we understand it anyway, means that you love your brother, defend him, help him ... and never miss an opportunity to beat him in some sort of competition. Such as the aforementioned tractors. We have an ongoing tractor fight, which we both enjoy. Immensely.

It started when he and I went to a tractor show in Ohio and I bought a die-cast model of an Oliver Row Crop 60. Why? Because our grandfather had an Oliver Row Crop 60. That's all I was thinking at the time: Grandpa's tractor. That little model took me right back to my kidhood, sitting on the back steps, watching Grandpa chug in from the field at lunchtime, his brown fedora on his head, his chrome-stemmed Falcon pipe clenched between his teeth. I loved my grandfather, so I bought the tractor.

I brought it home and put it on a shelf, and when P.D. called a few weeks later to say that he, too, had bought a model of an Oliver 60, I was pleased. I do like to set a good example, you know.

Then he called again a few weeks later to report that he had also picked up a model of an Oliver 1850. Our Uncle John had an 1850, which, when we first saw it back in the 1960s, looked to us like the biggest tractor on the face of the earth. The view from its seat felt like looking down from a second-story window.

I mean, it was *huge*. Or so we thought. Compared to some of those monsters I see on display at the state fair every year, it's a garden tractor.

At any rate, P.D. had a model of one and, as he pointed out, at some length, I did not. Ah, but a few weeks later, I was able to call him back and report that I had an Oliver Row Crop 77. This was Grandpa's other tractor, his "big" tractor. Well, we thought it was big until we saw Uncle John's 1850. Which just goes to show you that size matters after all.

The 77 was the tractor Grandpa was driving in our favorite photo of him, and so I sensed a bit of irritation in my brother's voice when I told him I had picked up this little gem. Well, actually, not in his voice, because the conversation went something like this:

(Ring ring ring)

P.D.: Hello?

Mike: Got a model of an Oliver Row Crop 77, narrow front?

P.D.: No.

Mike: I do. Ha ha ha ha ha ha ha ha.

Which is when he hung up.

But—and this ought to show you what a splendid big brother I really am—what he did not know was that I had purchased not one, but *two*, count 'em, two Oliver 77s. And I gave him the second one for Christmas. Of course, by that time I had also picked up an Oliver 70 and a Cletrac (made by Oliver) crawler. And by that time he had done the same, and raised me a Super 77 diesel.

I saw his Super 77 and added a Super 44. He saw the 44 and raised me a Row Crop 88. I saw the 88. And then I raised him with what I thought would be the game-winner.

Most of our tractors, you see, had been in the twenty-five to one hundred dollar range. But one day while walking through the mall I happened to look in one of those collectibles stores—you know, the place where you can get the Harley-Davidson pocketknife and the John Wayne gas pump and other frightfully expensive stuff that really makes no sense, when you think about it. I mean, who needs a non-firing replica of a Winchester rifle with pictures of Marilyn Monroe, James Dean, and Elvis Presley carved into the stock?

Anyway, sitting on a pedestal there was a large model of what I believe was the greatest tractor Oliver ever produced: The Super 99 Diesel. In its day, the mid- to late 1950s, it was as powerful a tractor as had ever been produced.

P.D. and I had seen only one of these tractors in our lives—at that show in Ohio. It was during the Parade Of Iron that was the highlight of the show. A line of nothing but old Oliver tractors passed before a county fair grandstand, one great old model after another, and then the announcer paused for dramatic effect.

"And now …" he said, as the crowd edged forward on the plank seats of the grandstand, "… the Super 99 Diesel!"

The driver rolled his tractor—big, brutish, green—up to the track. He dropped it down into a lower gear, eased off the clutch, and yanked open the throttle. Dense black blasts of diesel smoke burst from the stacks as the big rear tires began digging into the fairground's clay. And then came the sound—a roar so deep and powerful that you felt it hitting you in the chest a split second before it crashed into your ears.

What a thrill. Hats and babies flew into the air. Women fanned themselves with their programs. Strong men wept. To a couple of tractor geeks like P.D. and me, it was goosebump time.

"Wow," I said.

"Yeah," said P.D.

Maybe you had to be there.

Anyway, here I was walking through the mall and there sat an absolutely perfect model of that very same tractor. It was big, too, at least twice the size of the other tractors in my collection, detailed down to the last spark plug wire and hydraulic hose. And it was expensive, at least twice what I had paid for the most expensive tractor in my collection. No matter. I had to have it.

The phone call to P.D. that night was short and sweet.

(Ring ring ring)

P.D.: Hello?

Mike: Super 99 Diesel. Perfectly detailed.

P.D.: Where?

Mike: Right here in front of me.

P.D.: I mean, where'd you get it?

Mike: A store. Gotta go. Bye.

(Click)

Of course, I knew it would only be a matter of time before P.D. went to the World Wide Web and stumbled onto the information he needed. He did not disappoint me. He called back twenty minutes later.

(Ring ring ring)

Mike: Hello?

P.D.: Got one.

(Click)

Of course, since he had to wait for his to be delivered, that still put me ahead of him for two or three days. Just to make sure, I went online and ordered my own 1850, like Uncle John's, and an Oliver 70 with steel wheels instead of rubber. By my count, this kept me in the lead.

What I liked best about the competition was that it was all-Oliver. My interest in Oliver tractors was more than just simple nostalgia for Grandpa. Oliver was a company with a rich Indiana history, beginning in South Bend as the Oliver Chilled Plow Works. In 1929, the Oliver plow works merged with Hart-Parr Tractor Company of Charles City, Iowa; the Nichols and Shepard Threshing Machine Company of Battle Creek, Michigan; and the American Seeding Machine Company of Springfield, Ohio, and the Oliver Farm Equipment Company was born.

Olivers had a reputation for being technologically advanced. They were the first tractors with independent power take-off, electric control of hydraulics, equalizer brake pedals, and double-disc brakes. They were beautiful, too— meadow green (a bluer shade than the green used for a certain other tractor with the initials J.D.) with red wheels and yellow trim. The Fleetlines, of which Grandpa's 77 was a prime example, were renowned for their sleek, aerodynamic design.

Unfortunately, all that innovation came to naught in the 1960s. White Motor Corporation bought Oliver and did well enough with it for a few years, but by the early 1970s, the Oliver nameplate was as dead as Hupmobile. And now the only big green tractor you see anymore is that other brand, John Deere, which probably makes as much in a year of selling collectibles as Oliver made in ten of selling tractors.

Grandpa and Uncle John were dedicated Oliver owners. I once asked Uncle John what it was about the Oliver that caught Grandpa's fancy, and kept it. The

Continental engines? That power take-off? The hydraulics? The brakes?

"The seat," said Uncle John. "Oliver had the most comfortable seats."

Oh.

Well, at least P.D. and I were dedicated to the tractor that meant the most to our Grandpa's rear end.

Until P.D. changed the rules, that is.

We were at the State Fair, looking at the old tractors up near the Pioneer Pavilion, when my brother ducked away for a few minutes. I figured he was making a lemonade run or something, but when he came back it wasn't a drink he had in his hands. It was a toy tractor.

A Farmall.

"What are you doing with *that*?" I demanded.

"I always liked that Farmall M," he said. "I drove one when I worked for Tom." Tom was our neighbor.

"But it's not an Oliver."

"I know that."

"We're supposed to collect Olivers."

"Says who? I wasn't aware we had rules about this."

"Of course we do. We're Oliver collectors. You can't just go and get a Farmall because you drove one once."

"I *liked* that tractor. Besides, it's my collection. I'm collecting tractors that mean something to me. I saw an Allis-Chalmers like the one Uncle Maurice used to have and I'm thinking about buying it. And there's a Minneapolis-Moline like the one I drove when I worked for Donald DePue. Oh, and remember that Case you drove when you worked for Bob Atkinson? Saw one. You ought to get it."

I couldn't believe what I was hearing. Yes, I did drive a Case once and I liked it, but that didn't mean I was going to put it in among my precious Olivers. I have my integrity, you know. Unlike my brother, who does not follow the rules.

He says his collection is larger because it has more tractors. That may be true, technically, but mine is pure Olivers. It's a question of quality over quantity. Or maybe I was wrong about the size thing. It doesn't matter after all.

Which, now that I think about it, is a discussion I'd just as soon not get into with my brother.

What we have here, really, is an illustration of the two sides of the extended family dynamic shared by we siblings. P.D., in this case, represents the happy-go-lucky Redmond side: *What's the difference? They're all tractors, aren't they? Besides, they all mean something to me. If you don't approve, we can always step outside.* My attitude is more typical of the McKenzie side: *We have rules and they are to be followed. Oliver tractors are clearly superior. Without some sort of structure, the collection becomes meaningless. If you don't approve, we can always step outside.*

Anyone who grew up in a family where one side is Irish and the other is Scottish knows exactly what I mean. The Irish Redmonds are like jazz musicians. They're improvisers. Sometimes it works and sometimes it doesn't, but it's always interesting. The Scottish McKenzies, on the other hand, are more like symphony players. They stick to what's on the page, but they play it beautifully, and note-perfect, every time. Each has its merits, of course, just as each has its faults: The Redmond side tends to be a little irresponsible, at least to a McKenzie. And the McKenzie side tends to be a little rigid, at least to a Redmond.

When we were kids, I tended to identify more with the Redmond side and P.D. seemed more in the McKenzie camp. As we've gotten older, we seem to have moved to the middle and now we draw from each side in more or less equal measures, which strikes me as the best way to go about the business of dealing with your family tree. Unless, of course, you are talking about toy tractors, in which case I am right and P.D. is dead wrong.

Which, by the way, is a very McKenzie thing of me to say.

Over the years I may have created the impression that P.D. and I compete all the time. This isn't true. In fact, I defer to my brother quite a bit on areas where his expertise is greater than mine, such as … well, give me a minute. No, I'm kidding. In the areas of construction, home improvement, and general handyman work, I always defer to my brother because he's better at it than me. Most of the time.

P.D. has the skills, the tools, and most important the confidence to get in and tackle projects of all types and sizes. I tend to be a little more tentative. A home improvement project for me usually requires careful study of six or seven how-to books, two or three trips to the hardware store, and at least one solid day of standing there screwing up the courage to get in and get started. After which I usually screw up something else, and have to call P.D. to tell me how to fix it.

But my brother does have one handyman failing. He tends to take the long way around a problem. Like a couple of years ago when he was building brooder boxes for a bunch of chicks we were having shipped up to the farm in La-Grange County.

Now, for those of you who haven't been around chickens, a little explanation: Baby chicks have to be kept warm, and since they only sit under mother hens in cartoons (all our chicks come from a hatchery; as far as they're concerned, their mother is a cardboard box), you need a brooder. The most common way to provide a source of heat is with a light bulb, which has to be adjustable in some way so that the temperature can be regulated. If the brooder is too cold, the chicks freeze. And if it's too hot, you have the world's teeniest rotisserie chickens.

So my brother calls me and tells me he has an idea for moving the light bulb up and down so as to create the optimum condition for the birds. He wants to rig up some elaborate Rube Goldberg system involving a chain and sprockets from an old Murray bicycle, a seat belt and shoulder harness from a Honda Civic, two sections of throttle linkage from a lawnmower, the belt drive from a rototiller, seventeen feet of garden hose, a hydraulic jack, and the electric motor off the refrigerator, if Mom doesn't mind going out and buying a new fridge to replace the one he wants to cannibalize.

"Uh … why don't you just attach the light to a piece of wire and raise or lower it as you need?" I asked.

P.D. paused.

"Well, I guess that would work," he said.

I have never forgotten that moment, and neither will he, because I won't let him.

As kids, P.D. and I often presented a formidable tag-team challenge to our sister Vicky who, as mom's trusted lieutenant (or, as we preferred, brown-nosing snitch), was frequently left in charge of us.

When Vicky left to go to college, the job of being Mom's second-in-command fell to me, and I like to think I was a little easier on my brother. I like to think that, but it's not true. Mom had appointed me her sergeant-at-arms, her enforcer, and I approached the job with what we shall call enthusiasm. In fact, because of this enthusiasm my brother did not eat peas until well into his adult years. As in a couple of years ago.

(You should know this about my brother: He has weird eating habits. He'll get on something he likes and eat it every day until he gets sick of it. Which in some cases means he can go for months with the same food on his plate every day. In our family, for example, we often refer to the calendar year 1968 as "The Year P.D. Ate Nothing But Bacon-Lettuce-And-Tomato Sandwiches."

He also develops aversions to certain foods for reasons that are unrelated to the food itself. Honey, for example. P.D. did not eat honey for three solid years (1965, 1966, and 1967). Why? Because in the spring of '65, he was stung by a bee, and so that was it for P.D. and honey. I said he was being weird. P.D. said he was trying to teach the bees a lesson.

Which gets us to what history has recorded as the Pea Patch Incident.)

We had rather a large vegetable garden, and we boys shared the responsibility of keeping it nice and clean, which is why it usually looked like a vacant lot. In LaGrange County, where a neat garden is seen as a reflection of your worth as a human being, this caused our mother no small embarrassment.

One summer the pea patch was in particularly bad shape. In fact, it didn't look like a pea patch at all. It rather favored the set of a Tarzan movie, and not one of the good Johnny Weissmuller Tarzan movies, either. We're talking low-budget jungle here, full of lambsquarter and burdock. Oh, and thistles, which, if you are Tarzan running around in nothing but a loincloth, is a weed you do not want to know about up close and personally.

P.D. had gotten on Mom's bad side for something, and to punish him he was sent out there to weed the peas, all by himself, at eight A.M. At nine, Mom looked out the kitchen window and saw him just sitting in the weeds, pouting. Same thing at ten. Also at eleven.

By 11:15 she had had enough.

"Mike," she said, "get out there and make your brother weed those peas."

I trooped dutifully out to the garden and my sulking brother.

"Mom says to weed the peas," I said.

"No," he responded.

Back to the house I went.

"He said no," I reported.

"Tell him I said he'd better or else," said Mom.

Back to the garden, where my brother remained pretty much as I had left him a couple of minutes earlier.

"Mom said you'd better, or else," I said.

"Or else what?"

Back to the house.

"He wants to know or else what," I told Mom, who was vacuuming the living room.

"Or else he'll regret it," she said, calling over her shoulder as an errant Hot Wheels car, chased from under the sofa, went clattering up the intake tube of our Electrolux.

I once again went back to the garden, following the path I was starting to wear into the grass.

"She says or else you'll regret it," I said.

"Tell her I don't care. I don't even like peas. Why should I have to weed them if I don't even eat them?"

I had to admit he had logic on his side. And with that I turned and headed once more to the house.

Mom didn't even let me say anything.

"You get *back* out there and make your brother weed those peas," she said. "I don't care how. Beat him up if you have to, but somebody is going to weed those peas, and if you can't make him do it, then it is going to be you."

Now I was a man on a mission: Operation Make P.D. Weed The Peas Because I Sure Don't Want To. Back to the garden one more time.

"Mom says if you don't weed the peas I am supposed to beat you up," I said, which, while not a verbatim quote, gave him what I felt to be the salient point of Mom's message.

"I'm not weeding the peas," my brother said.

Well, nobody accused the kid of being bright. I sailed into him.

He was game, I'll give him that. We were just about the same size at this point, and he answered my haymakers with a few pretty good shots of his own. He almost rang my bell a couple of times. Almost.

I went back at him with a renewed sense of urgency. This time the kid was no match for me and he knew it. And so he decided he had better do something to negate my advantage. He reached into his pocket and pulled out a knife.

Now, truth be told, it wasn't much of a knife. It had cost him a buck at the drug store. It had one cutting blade which, to my knowledge, had never been sharpened, and one fish-scaling blade. They were both covered with as much rust as a knife can accumulate in four years of neglect, which is to say quite a bit. In fact, he couldn't even get it open.

As he stood there, hunched over at the waist, grunting and straining and trying to get the blade's oxidized hinge to give up its grip, I looked around for something I might use to dissuade him. My eyes settled on a hoe. I picked it up by the shovel end, raised the handle over my head, and brought it down squarely on his hands. So much for the fish knife.

My brother disarmed, I went after him again, and this time I was taking no prisoners. I knocked him down, flipped him onto his stomach and grabbed him by the back of the head. I then proceded to dig a hole in the pea patch, using his nose for the shovel.

My brother was limp as a dishrag when I left him to go back into the house. It was, after all, lunchtime.

I was sitting there eating my tomato soup and grilled cheese sandwich when P.D. came in. His face was black with dirt. He went upstairs, where Mom had taken the Electrolux, to wash up.

A couple of minutes later I heard my mother's voice:

"MICHAEL JAMES REDMOND! YOU GET UP HERE RIGHT AWAY!"

Uh-oh. She used all three names, and we all know what that means. Trouble. Big trouble. *Felony* trouble.

It seems my mother had watched as my brother went into the bathroom to wash his face. She watched as the layers of topsoil ran down the bathroom drain … except for the black around his eyes.

I had given my brother a double shiner. Two beauts, plus the bridge of his nose. He looked like he was wearing a mask. Which my mother was dabbing gently with a cool washcloth while my brother hammed it up with moans and groans.

"Look what you did to your brother!" she said. "My God! Two black eyes! I've never seen anything like it! What on earth made you *do* this?"

"Uh, you did," I said.

Wrong answer.

"I did no such thing!" she yelled, chasing me back downstairs, smacking me about the head and shoulders with the tube from the Electrolux.

"You did too!" I hollered back as I tried to stay out of range. "You said I should beat him up if I had to, and I had to!"

"Out! Out! Outside!" she yelled as we moved away from the stairs, down the hallway, and into the kitchen. "And don't you even think about coming back in here until those peas are weeded, do you hear me?"

I stood there for a minute, dumbfounded. I had no idea that I wasn't supposed to take my mother literally on the beating-up thing. All my life she had been telling me that when she gave me an order she expected it to be carried out to the letter. Now, suddenly, the rules changed because my stupid brother wouldn't weed the peas and I tried to make him—in the way that had been, if not ordered, at least suggested by my mother?

It was just too weird.

And so I did the only thing I could think of to do.

I trudged back out to the garden and started weeding the peas.

Wouldn't it be nice if life were like the movies? If life were like the movies, I could say that a short while after I got started P.D. came out and without a word started to help me pull all that burdock and lambsquarter and thistle out of the pea patch. I could say that out of the Pea Patch Incident we grew to respect each other and take the first steps toward the close relationship we enjoy today. I could say that we truly began to become brothers that day.

But life, as we know, is very seldom like the movies.

I stayed out there weeding peas for about seven straight hours while P.D. watched through a window. Well, actually, he only watched me part of the time. The rest of the time he was putting ice packs on his face and giving me the finger, although he did the finger business only when he knew Mom wasn't looking.

It took a few years more for all that brotherly love jazz to start kicking in. I think it really began in earnest after my brother, his friend Larry Peters, and our cousin Kent Sunday moved to Houston to seek their fortunes in the late 1970s. They didn't find them, by the way.

Instead they found low-paying jobs (Kent and Larry as security guards at a refinery, P.D. as a reporter for a dinky little neighborhood newspaper). P.D. and Larry found an apartment at a grubby apartment complex in a grubby suburb (a gruburb?) where the cockroaches outnumbered the humans about 400 million to one. And they learned to subsist on the cheapest provender available at their local foodliner: hot dogs and chicken pot pies, and not even the store brand. I'm talking the ones in the white packages with plain black letters. Generic hot dogs. Or, as P.D. called them in a letter home, "snouts and eyeballs in a tube." Oh, yum.

The family, alarmed by further reports from P.D.'s letters ("You should have seen the shooting outside our front window last night"), dispatched me to Texas to check up on him. I arrived to find that if anything, P.D. had shown himself to be fairly good at understatement. The roaches actually outnumbered the humans about 800 million to one.

I took a look at the boys and then at their refrigerator and quickly came to the conclusion that what they needed most was a decent meal. And so off I went to Kroger.

Four hours later I was in the kitchen, frying chicken. Actually, the trip to the store only took about thirty minutes, but it took me three and a half hours to get the kitchen looking less like a landfill and into some semblance of a decent cooking area. And as I cooked I was aware of two people watching me closely— Larry standing on my right taking deep sniffs, and P.D. standing on my left watching to see how I did it.

There wasn't much talk at the dinner table that night. The boys were too busy inhaling their food. They swept up four chickens and five pounds of mashed potatoes in just under ten minutes. Even the cockroaches were astonished. And mad. There wasn't even a crumb left for them.

That was the first time I can recall taking care of my brother, in the nurturing sense of the phrase. And I do think it was what began to shift us into the adult mode of our brotherhood.

The shift was complete a few years later when I was in the throes of a deep depression and P.D.—who had by then moved to Central Indiana to work at the newspaper in Franklin—got me through one bad night when I thought I should just crawl inside a bottle of scotch and stay there. Even through that alcoholic fog, I was aware of him calling Mom and Dad to ask what he should do, and then quietly moving through my house, removing all the alcohol. He took care of me.

Now we are friends, best friends. When something good happens to me, or something bad, and I need to tell someone, my brother is the first person who comes to mind.

There is no one I would rather see sitting across from me at a partnership pinochle game. Nobody I would rather pitch horseshoes with at the family reunion. Nobody I would rather just hang out with, talking and laughing.

Of course, we still compete. We're brothers. It's part of our makeup to try to best each other: Which one is first to grill outside each year (P.D., who always manages to burn at least *one* batch of brats in the middle of a snowstorm); who has the better library of comic books (me, although that's in some dispute because I prefer DC books and P.D. likes Marvel); who has more DVDs (a dead heat at the moment).

But where work is concerned, there's no longer any need for me to be Mom's enforcer or for P.D. to be enforced. He has a small plot of vegetables at the home place, tending it on weekends when he comes over from his job at a television station in Toledo, and he keeps it pretty clean. Including the peas, which he now eats with gusto.

My brother really is the one person I can trust, the one person I can count on when the chips are down, the one person to whom I can confide my secrets and confess my fears. I know he'll be there to listen to me and support me, and at a price much cheaper than that charged by my therapist.

It's just too bad he's so wrong about those tractors.

FIVE

Great Dogs

I have known lots of good dogs in my life. Most dogs, to my way of thinking, are good dogs. They exhibit qualities I admire: Loyalty, intelligence, cheerfulness, bravery, thrift, reverence … oh, wait. That's Boy Scouts. Well, except for the thrift, it's dogs, too.

Good dogs are good pals, and it has been that way since the first wolf wandered up to the first caveman and said, "Hello. If you give me something to eat I will guard your family and your home, sleep next to you to keep you warm, give you someone to talk to in the middle of the night, watch television with you once you invent it, and also not rip your leg to shreds. How about it? Do we have a deal?"

My dog Cookie is a good dog. She's friendly, she's funny, and most of all she thinks I am the center of the universe. The latter is not a quality I seek in relationships, inter-personal *or* inter-species, but I won't refuse it when offered.

I don't yet know if Cookie will graduate from being a good dog to a great dog. She's just four years old, so it's too early to tell. At just four she still, as we dog owners like to say, "has a lot of puppy in her." This is dog-owner code for, "She still acts like a moron most of the time." But I hold out hope that with time and more training and time and maturity and most of all time, Cookie may someday join the pantheon of Great Dogs I Have Known.

The greatest of these, hands down, was my Grandpa's dog Hoss, and I am not alone in this opinion. You can ask any of us McKenzie cousins and we will tell you that Hoss was the greatest dog ever to walk the face of the planet, and we will not entertain discussion on the matter.

Hoss was a fawn-colored terrier mix, about thirty-five pounds I guess, with soft brown eyes, tipped ears, and a mouth that always seemed to be in a grin. When he barked, he didn't say "woof" or "bow-wow" or any of those other things dogs are alleged to say. Hoss said "york." You'd pull into Grandma and Grandpa's long driveway and Hoss would come running out to greet you, york-ing all the way.

Hoss was famous in LaGrange County for his ability to ride on moving vehicles. Not in. On. Grandpa's tractor, for instance. Hoss loved to ride on the tractor. The problem was, there isn't much space on a tractor for a dog to ride, so one day my Uncle Verl solved that by attaching an old manger box to the side of the tractor and teaching Hoss to ride in that. We called it the Hoss Box. What else are you going to call it? Years later, long after they had both passed away, people would come up to me and tell me about how they once saw Hoss riding on the tractor with Grandpa.

Hoss also rode on Uncle Verl's Indian motorcycle. For years, I thought I had imagined this, but a couple of family reunions ago I ran it past Uncle Verl and he said no, I wasn't dreaming. I really *did* see Hoss sitting there on the tank of Uncle Verl's bike as it came into the driveway.

"Not only that," my uncle said, "but he leaned with the turns. Most dogs, you know, if they're on something that leans like a motorcycle, their instinct is to lean the other way, but not Hoss. He leaned with the bike."

That, my friends, is the sign of a great dog. There are people who ride on motorcycles who aren't smart enough to lean with the turn.

But I think the measure of Hoss' true greatness was in his calm dog demeanor. There are fifty of us McKenzie cousins, and that meant for much of his dog life, Hoss was surrounded by kids, some of whom were too young to know that it isn't nice to pull a dog's ears, or bite his tail, or drool on him. And not once did Hoss so much as mumble a note of disapproval.

Hoss loved all of us kids, and we knew it. Take the time my cousin Eldon had done something wrong. His dad, Uncle Eldon, was giving him a spanking in Grandma and Grandpa's living room. Hoss heard the commotion and was across the room like a shot. He jumped up, grabbed Uncle Eldon by the wrist, and gave him one of those "lay off this kid or you will answer to me" growls. Hoss became a hero that day to an entire generation of McKenzies.

Actually, all my Grandfather's dogs were great dogs. The ones who came before me—most notably, Clarence and Glenn—I have only heard about. At the same reunion, Uncle Verl was talking about Clarence, who was accidentally killed when he ran in front of Grandpa's truck while racing it home for lunch, as he did every day.

"And even as he lay there and he was dying, his tail was wagging," Uncle Verl said. "He was looking up at us and it was like he was saying, 'I beat you. I beat you.'" His eyes filled with tears and his voice thickened. "Dammit, that was fifty years ago and look, it still chokes me up," he said.

I should tell you about Grandpa's dog-naming protocol: His dogs were always named after the person who gave him the dog. Glenn, for example, was named for Glenn Troyer, the bread man, who came around one day with a box of rat terrier puppies among the whites and whole wheats, and left one at the McKenzie place.

Hoss got his name when Aunt Sharon found him at the place where she worked. Since there wasn't a person to name him after, Grandpa named him after the place instead. And that is why Hoss's real name was Hospital.

I don't know where Victor's name came from, but I do know that Victor is a dog whose name still inspires reverence in those who knew him.

He was a border collie-German shepherd cross—marked like a border, but with the greater size of the shepherd. And he was, hands down, the smartest dog anyone ever saw.

Victor used to bring the cows in from the field to be milked, every day. At the exact same time. Without being told.

And when you wanted to separate a cow from the herd, you had merely to point at it, and Victor would take it from there.

Uncle Verl again:

"Dad had some cows he wanted to sell, and when the livestock man came there he asked us where to put the truck. We said to drive it right into the barnyard. He looked at us kind of funny, but he did it.

"We got in there and told him to put the ramp down. Then I just stood there and pointed to the cow that Dad wanted to sell. Victor looked at me, looked at my hand, and then cut that cow out of the herd and ran it right up that ramp. I didn't even have to say anything to him.

"Well, do you know that livestock man came back every day for a week trying to buy that dog? 'I've got to have that dog,' he'd say, and every day he came back he'd offer one hundred dollars more for him. By the end of the week he was offering one thousand dollars for Victor, but Dad wouldn't sell."

Grandpa did, eventually, sell all the cows, though, which would have meant retirement for a lesser dog. Not Victor. He simply refocused his talents into herding the pigs instead—which, in fact, requires a whole different set of dog skills. He liked nothing more than to chase the pigs into the barn and go from one side of the herd to the other by running across their backs.

Nope, for sheer doggie smarts, Victor was hard to top.

But all my Grandpa's dogs were smart. The reason, I am sure, is because they had a smart master who spent eighteen hours a day with them. Grandpa loved his dogs and treated them well; they loved him back and tried to please him.

Not that they didn't have their quirks.

Bow, for example. Bow was a beagle who broke the naming pattern, being christened instead for a bow-shaped white patch on the back of his neck. True to his beagle ancestry, Bow was quite a traveling man. We used to see him wandering around the town of Brighton in the evenings. That's three miles from Grandma and Grandpa's house. I guess Bow had a girlfriend.

Bow also had an appetite for corn. Lucky for him, it grew in abundance on all sides of the house, so all he had to do was walk out into the field and pick an ear. Which he did. Got up on his hind legs, grabbed it with his teeth and pulled it right off the stalk. Then he'd bring it back to the yard, strip off the husks, and munch away.

We had a variety of dogs at our place. We had Sheldon, a collie-shepherd mix who was, in fact, female. P.D. and I just thought Sheldon was a funny name for a dog. We had Sam, a sweet black mutt who wandered up one day and decided to stay, and who earned Mom's undying gratitude by single-handedly ridding the yard of moles (although when he finished, the yard looked like the battlefield from *Sergeant York*).

We had Casey, an Irish water spaniel who was dumped along the Indiana Toll Road by people who didn't realize he was a purebred. They thought he was just some sort of weird poodle.

We had Jack, my brother's border collie who could turn on a dime and give you seven cents' change; we had Eva, a blue tick hound-beagle cross I found and kept a few weeks before giving her to people who, to my everlasting regret, renamed her Binky. And we had Arthur. Of all these dogs, the only one we really talk about when we get together is Arthur. Arthur was our family's great dog.

Arthur was supposed to be a Manchester terrier. I say supposed to be because it was obvious there was more than Manchester terrier in the family tree. He had the head of a Manchester, and the markings of one, but a squat little fireplug body that indicated the presence of a dachshund, perhaps, in the genetic code. Or a pig. Mom said he looked like a pinhead. Harsh, but accurate.

Arthur was the pup of two dogs named Norma and Timmy. Timmy later gained a measure of fame for a most spectacular exit from this plane of existence. It seems he and his owners were on vacation in the Great Smoky Mountains and stopped at one of those scenic overlooks to scan the scenery and let Timmy do his business. While the folks were looking at the mountains, Timmy hiked a leg to leave a message for the next dog to come along. Trouble is, he had wandered a little too close to the edge and … you guessed it. He lost his footing. Down he went hundreds of feet, writing all the way. It said "Timmy Was Here," in very large letters, I presume.

There is some dispute in the family over how the son of Timmy and Norma came to be named Arthur. My brother will tell you he thought of it. This is a big, fat lie. Our little sister Amy, who was three, named Arthur.

The night we brought him home, she was watching an episode of *Family Affair* (although not the one where, late at night when the children are asleep, Mr. French does unspeakable things to Mrs. Beasley.) On this show, the little boy, Jody, has an imaginary pet bear named Arthur. Amy liked the show and so Arthur became the name of our new dog.

Actually, it doesn't matter much because Amy quickly shortened his name to "Arfy," which became "Arf." And "Arf" is what he went by most of his life.

He was a smart dog, as terriers are, and a strong-willed one, also as terriers are. I'm thinking of the time the veterinarian said Arf had been tucking into the chow a bit too enthusiastically. He was getting a little chunky, Dr. Tetrick said, and we ought to switch him to a diet dog food.

Mom went out and bought a bag of Purina Fit & Trim. She poured some into Arthur's bowl and watched as he came up, sniffed at it, and promptly turned up his nose. Now, keep in mind that this is a dog, an animal that likes to eat garbage and roll in dead things. When a dog turns up his nose at a bowl of food, you know you've either got unbelievably bad food or an unbelievably strong-willed dog. I knew Arf, so I'm going with the latter.

Later that evening, Mom hit on what she thought was a solution: Bacon grease. That was Arthur's preferred condiment. He liked it on his pancakes in the morning and on his popcorn in the evening. Not pausing to think that there really wasn't much point in serving your dog diet food if you were just going to douse it in pork fat, Mom spooned some bacon grease onto Arthur's chow. No reaction.

No reaction until later that night, however, when we heard the familiar sound of Arthur rustling around in his bowl. Then we heard a strange clattering noise. P.D. and I went out to the kitchen to see Arthur standing at his bowl, picking up pieces of chow one at a time, rolling them around in his mouth to get at the grease, and then spitting the kibble—ptoo—onto the floor.

Arthur's weight came from fondness for anything other than dog food. Caramels, for instance. He loved caramels. Have you ever seen a dog eat a caramel? It's kind of like when your Grandma's dentures come unglued while she's ... well, eating a caramel. It's not pretty. It is, however, funny.

And pecans. Arthur loved pecans so much we couldn't leave them out in the nut dish. I'm talking about pecans with shells on them, too. He'd root around in the bowl until he found one he liked and then crack it, dig out the nutmeat and spit out that bitter paper, and leave the shells on the floor. He usually did this in the middle of the night while the rest of us were sleeping, and it was not uncommon for us to come downstairs the next day to find the sharp pieces of shell from five or six pecans on the living room floor. This is why, to this day, every person in my family puts on his or her shoes first thing in the morning.

Arthur's true calling in life was as a snake hunter. Our place is in a swampy, marshy area and there is no shortage of reptile life in the neighborhood, and when he was still a pup Arf took it upon himself to patrol the grounds every day looking for what he considered the enemy.

He wasn't a big dog—maybe twelve, fourteen inches tall—so he would disappear when he went into the tall grass on a snake hunt. You'd see the grass moving as Arthur snuffled around, seeking his prey. Then the grass would suddenly begin to rustle, violently, and in a few seconds you'd see a snake come flying out of there, looping end over end after being shaken and then thrown by twenty-five pounds of outraged mutt. Then Arthur would emerge from the grass, mission accomplished, ptooing all the way to the nearest puddle so he could get the taste of snake out of his mouth.

In a general sense, Arthur was the family dog, but he really belonged to three people: P.D., Amy, and Mom. He was P.D.'s buddy. They slept in the same room and went for car rides together. He was Amy's playmate, which meant he had to endure the occasional afternoon dressed up in doll clothes. P.D. and I happened to see him one afternoon in an outfit Amy had borrowed from an over-size Holly Hobby doll, including a darling little sunbonnet. The way Arthur looked at us—well, let's put it this way: Don't ever let anyone tell you that dogs can't be embarrassed.

But it was Mom who taught Arthur his manners, taught him his tricks (using hamburger as the incentive, because Arthur would do anything for a bite of hamburger; he was a hamburger whore), and Mom whom Arthur chose to be with when he had nothing else, such as car rides or snake hunts, on his agenda.

Mom generally didn't mind his company except for one place: the bathroom. I agree with her on this one. There are certain places you just don't need a dog with you, and that one is near the top of the list. Not that Arthur felt the same. If Mom went into the bathroom, Arthur generally followed right behind. And then she kicked him out.

He took to sitting at the top of the stairs to wait for her. She'd come out and Arthur would go back downstairs to do whatever it was he planned to do next. Eventually he refined his timing even further and would start back down the stairs when he heard the toilet paper being unrolled.

Everybody loved Arthur except Dad. I still don't why that was, except that Dad was, in the words of my brother, "a sucker for a pedigree." Maybe you know people like this. They choose their dogs like they are buying shoes, based on whatever breed catches their fancy when they watch a dog show on TV: "Well, the dachshund is so *last year*, you know. We rather thought we'd go with something in the Norwich terrier line for fall."

Dad preferred large, purebred dogs. Such as Duke, the Labrador he brought home who was, to put it mildly, dumb as dirt. As in didn't know his own name. Well, that was the impression one got, anyway, after watching him drag Dad around the yard while Dad yelled, "Duke! Stop! Heel! Down! Duke! Duke!" But Dad insisted Duke was descended from Dog Royalty and had only to settle down a bit before he became a Noble Companion and Loyal Protector. Then

Duke ate one of the seats from Dad's Opel GT and that was it for Duke.

Dad never really gave Arf much of a break, until the day my brother P.D. was mowing the lawn and ran over a piece of wire that rocketed toward the house and hit Arf. It was Dad who threw Arthur into the car and drove like a bat out of hell to the veterinarian's office twelve miles away (P.D. says they made it in about eight minutes). Maybe Dad cared more than he let on, or maybe he did it because he knew how *we* felt about the dog. At any rate, despite years of ignoring him, Dad came through for Arf in the pinch, and that counts for something.

After I left home to make my way in the world, I lived a mostly dogless life. I liked dogs, but I didn't feel I had time to make a good home for one. Dogs require attention and companionship, and I was busy being a Soaring Young Comet of Journalism and Man About Town. In other words, I was too selfish to have a dog.

As I matured I did, however, pick up a couple of cats, Molly and Bess. Molly died a few years ago but Bess is with me still, sitting a few inches from me as I type this, in fact. I like having cats in the house. They're beautiful and occasionally hilarious. I used to wait eagerly for nine o'clock to roll around every night, because at nine o'clock some sort of switch would go off in Molly's and Bess's cat brains, and they would go absolutely insane—running up and down stairs, jumping at things that weren't there, racing along the back of the sofa, skidding on the linoleum floor in the kitchen. And then, just as abruptly as they started, they would stop, and look at me as if *I* was the one who had just acted like a maniac.

Cats suited me, somehow. They were aloof. They gave affection only on their terms, and withdrew it at a moment's notice, with no explanation. They were just as likely to hiss at you as purr. Their allegiance to you was directly related to whatever you could do for them, such as empty the litter box or fill the food dish. In other words, having cats was a lot like having a girlfriend, only cheaper.

Somewhere along the line, however, I began to sense that a dog would be right for me. My work circumstances had changed and I was spending a lot more time at home. I liked the idea of a loyal dog curled up at my feet while I smoked my pipe and read in the evening. I liked the idea of a big, slobbery mutt greeting me when I came home. I liked the idea of going for rides in my pickup with my dog hanging its head out the window.

I happened to mention this to the vet, Trish Wiggers—just my sort of vague desire to have a dog, breed to be determined, someday in the future—when I had one of the cats in her office for an oil change and new spark plugs. A few weeks later, she called:

"I have your dog," said Trish.

I went down to the vet's office and she was right.

It was a little pup, mostly black with a white stripe running up her forehead. She looked, I thought, like an Oreo. As soon I picked her up, she licked my face and I was a goner. I had a dog. Because of the stripe on her head, I named her Cookie.

She was about seven weeks old then and had already had it rougher than she deserved. She came to Trish's office after being thrown out of a truck downtown. A woman saw this, scooped her up, and ran her directly to the vet for a checkup. And—I didn't learn this until much later—the woman was *also* calling the dog "Cookie," as in "Tough little …"

Trish and I could only guess what breeds were represented in Cookie's family tree. Because of her black-and-white markings, border collie seemed likely. Maybe some dalmation, given the preponderance of spots on her belly and chin. Labrador crossed our minds. So did greyhound. And because she was an urban dog, she could also have some pit bull terrier in there. Being unable to decide exactly what she was, and because she was one of the best examples I have ever seen of Puppy Clumsy—I mean, this dog would trip over the carpet—I decided that Cookie was a breed unto herself: American Doofus Hound.

Because we were unsure of her origins, we had no way of knowing what size dog Cookie would turn out to be. Trish put her years of veterinary training and practice to work and finally came up with an estimate: "I think she's going to be about a thirty-five-pound dog," she said. She only missed it by forty pounds.

By the way, I never for a minute believed Cookie would be a thirty-five-pound dog. I think Trish was going by the paw estimate, which I find to be unreliable. If you want to know how big your puppy is going to be, pay attention to the size of what comes out of the back end. At eight weeks old, Cookie was already dropping some heavy ordnance. I knew she was going to be a big girl.

The cats, needless to say, were outraged by Cookie's arrival. Which brings up an interesting question: Why, if something is needless to say, do we go ahead and say it? My theory is we like the sound of our own voices. But I guess that goes without saying.

Anyway, the cats immediately registered their displeasure at my bringing a Slobbering Barking Dumb Thing into the house. By which I mean I had to send the bedspread to the laundry several times those first few months, seeing as how I was getting little fragrant feline messages every other week or so. I really wish cats would find another way to let you know they are honked off. A postcard would be nice.

Cookie, for her part, seemed to think that hissing and a puffed-out tail were an invitation to play. Then again, Cookie seemed to think that everything was an invitation to play. "Here, Cookie" meant "Let's play." "Bad dog" meant "Let's play." The only thing that didn't seem to mean "Let's play" was "Let's play." If you said "Let's play" to Cookie, she was likely to go lie down.

Eventually we got that all straightened out with the help of obedience school. Cookie, I am proud to report, graduated third in her class, which is significantly better than I did in mine. Then again, there were only three dogs in her class. But the point is, she graduated, and I have the diploma to prove it, which is lucky, because you sure couldn't prove it by her behavior.

Cookie's main role in life, other than loving me, is to keep the yard clear of birds, squirrels, delivery persons, sticks, windblown trash, rocks, walnuts, and praying mantises. So far she has a spotless record on the sticks, trash, rocks, and walnuts. The delivery people don't seem to mind her one way or the other, and the other animals seem not to have gotten the message, even though Cookie has actually caught one bird (a lucky shot if I ever saw one—the dumb thing flew right at her), one squirrel (ditto), and one praying mantis (which, if Cookie's reaction is any indicator, was not exactly what you could call chock-full of mantis-y goodness; after she spit it out, I never saw a dog drink so much water).

The cats and Cookie have reached a détente of sorts. Basically, the cats get the upstairs of the house and Cookie gets the downstairs. Occasionally, very occasionally, you will see Cookie and one of the felines actually in the same room at the same time, but it never lasts long. One of them always wakes up.

Cookie, understand, does not wish to harm the cats. Any dog that can catch a squirrel can catch a cat, so I believe that if Cookie had mayhem in mind it would have happened by now. In her heart of hearts, she just wants to play. And in their heart of hearts, the cats are thinking dark things about me because I had them declawed.

Personally, I like having both dogs and cats in the house. You get different things from cats and dogs. Cats give your house beauty, grace, and the occasional hairball yakked squarely in the middle of the living room, usually when you are having company. For some reason, cats always seem to think hairballs should be as public as possible, the better, I guess, for us all to admire them.

From dogs you get loyalty, friendship, and passed gas. Also when you have company. Or when you are sleeping and the dog's tail is positioned somewhere near your pillow. That's Cookie's method, anyway.

Already my family is beginning to accumulate Cookie stories: How she ate a pound of millet birdseed (boy, did *that* make for some interesting botany in the back yard when, upon being delivered out the other end, the seed started sprouting); how she helped herself to the deli tray at a family party (was it her fault that her nose just happened to be the same height as the dining room table?); how she always adopts whomever comes to visit, meaning they get to sleep with a large dog in the guest bed whether they want to or not.

Whether my dog Cookie will ever achieve such legendary status as Hoss, Bow, Victor, or Arthur remains to be seen. She has a lot of goober in her, even for a dog. She makes a pest of herself at mealtime. She hogs the bed, and when a seventy-five-pound mutt hogs the bed, you can be sure the bed is well and truly hogged.

Oh, sure, she barks at strangers, but that's just to get their attention, and to tell you the truth, I am disinclined to correct her for it. You see, when you live downtown in a city, as I do, the panhandlers and hustlers occasionally save you the trouble of going to the street corners where they work, and instead come right to the door. I am not kidding.

Nine times out of ten, they tell me a hard-luck story involving their baby daughters (always daughters, never sons) and a desperate need for five bucks to buy (a.) diapers or (b.) hamburger. Once, when one of the guys told me he just needed to buy a little hamburger for his baby daughter, I went to the refrigerator and got some. Funny, he didn't want it. Guess it wasn't his brand.

At any rate, these guys (and yes, they're always guys) come to the door and Cookie just about has a conniption. She barks, she runs, she jumps up to try to see out the front door and acts, for all intents and purposes, as if she wants to take their legs off. Which could not be further from the truth.

All she wants is to be acknowledged. If they would pet her (not that they get close enough to do so; there's something about a loud dog that makes panhandlers quite speedy), they would learn that the barking is just Cookie's way of saying "I see you." If they would pet her, she would gladly give them a guided tour of the house and its contents. Including the place where I stash the valuables. Then she'd invite them to sit back, relax, watch a little TV.[1] She's no watchdog. She's just loud.

And she loves me. She loves everybody. As my brother P.D. observes, Cookie is a seventy-five-pound dog, but fifty pounds of it is heart. That, I think, may just be a great dog in the making.

---

[1]Television Shows For Dogs

Whose Butt Is It, Anyway?

Everybody Loves Garbage

Boneanza

I Spayed Lucy

What's My Breed?

Little House in the Backyard

The Scratch Game

SIX

Ride Your Glide

"Ride your glide, kids! Ride your glide!" I still hear those words in my sleep some-times, bellowed in a sandpaper voice that sounds exactly like Ma Kettle's as it echoes across the quiet shores of Cedar Lake in LaGrange County. "Ride your glide!"

The voice belonged to Elsie Shockley. "Ride your glide" was Elsie's way of telling her swimming students to slow down, take it easy, get the most use of each stroke, the way she did. Elsie was probably the world's slowest swimmer. Driftwood moved faster than Elsie, and she was proud of it.

I spent two summers at Cedar Lake in what was probably the best job of my life, working for Elsie at the Cedar Lake Swim School.

I wouldn't be a writer if I didn't have Elsie Shockley in my life, so blame her. Elsie got me my first newspaper job. There are some who think it's all been downhill from there, but I stopped listening to those uncles a long time ago.

Elsie did not own a newspaper. She just knew the right person to badger when I needed a job and that was the one I was interested in, and she went to bat for me. Elsie did that for a lot of people. She was an advocate before we knew what the word meant. But I'm getting ahead of myself.

I don't think there's any way of knowing just how many kids Elsie taught to swim at Cedar Lake. Viewed another way, there's no way to know how many drownings she prevented. I do know that just about every kid in the northern part of the county seemed to have learned to swim at Elsie's school, which was sort of a business she ran from her home. I say sort of a business because only a fraction of the kids took lessons that were actually paid for. She was retired from the Kirsch Company, a drapery hardware manufacturer up in Sturgis, Michigan, and the kids whose lessons were paid for were mostly children of Kirsch employees. The company picked up the tab. Elsie had arranged it with the big boss, Mr. Kirsch.

But hundreds, and I do mean hundreds, of other kids got their lessons at a reduced price, if not free, just because Elsie wanted them to know how to swim. Take a case from the first year I worked as a lifeguard for Elsie. After swim school was over for the day, you see, Elsie opened up her beach to the public. It was a generous thing to do, because Elsie owned one of the best swimming beaches in the area—a gravel bottom marked off by a U-shaped wooden pier, big enough to accommodate a hundred or so splashing kids. The Cedar Lake water was clear and cool, even on the hottest summer days, and the shady lot just up the hill from the beach gave parents a restful place where they could keep an eye on their kids. It was a great setup.

But Elsie's neighbors had covetous eyes where that beach was concerned, and so they began trumping up complaints about noise and bad behavior at the beach after school was over, trying to convince the county to shut it down and, I guess, force Elsie to sell to them. Elsie had no intention of giving them what they wanted, especially after she had taught all their kids to swim for free, and so she decided to fight back. Before, the beach had been a "swim at your own risk" place in the evenings. Now Elsie was spending her evenings there in addition to teaching at the school all day.

It was wearing her out. So one night, when I was there swimming with a couple of my cousins, I presented my credentials (Red Cross Water Safety Instructor, experienced babysitter, and owner of my own Acme Thunderer brand whistle) and told Elsie I'd be glad to keep an eye on the place in the evenings, just to give her a break and keep the neighbors off her back. She agreed, and so began one of the happiest associations of my life.

Elsie still spent much of the evening down at the beach, shooting the breeze with parents and helping me keep an eye on the kids—not that they really needed much attention. They were a pretty well-behaved bunch. All I really did was tell them not to run on the pier and keep the big kids from picking on the little ones.

One day, though, I got my test. Elsie and I were watching the kids from the little boathouse where she kept a refrigerator full of cold drinks, a small stack of life preservers, and a first aid kit. A man, I'd say in his early thirties, was there with a child of about six or so. He marched the kid out to the end of the pier, picked him up by the seat of the pants, threw him into the deep water and told the kid to start swimming. He was "teaching" his kid to swim.

The kid was screaming and sputtering and choking and most of all, not swimming. "Mike, go get him," Elsie said. I jogged down to the end of the pier, blowing my whistle because I figured it was the thing to do, to see if I could just reach out and grab the kid. No such luck. The dumbass had thrown him out of reach. Having nothing to toss to the kid and being pretty sure the kid was so panicked he wouldn't grab it if I did, I slipped off the pier, paddled about four strokes, and got an arm around the kid, who then proceeded to climb up said arm and try to perch on top of my head.

So I paddled back to the pier wearing the kid for a hat. I was just about to hand him up to someone when I looked up and there, flying over my head, went his father. And standing behind him was Elsie.

"Let's see how you like it!" she yelled.

Well, guess who else couldn't swim. I handed the kid over, grabbed the father, and hauled him in as well. Then I stood and glowered at him, in my best lifeguard manner, while Elsie read him the riot act about throwing his kid in the water. And believe me, when Elsie read you the riot act, she read you the riot act. Mothers clapped their hands over their children's ears, dogs hid under beds, grown men suddenly found something interesting to look at over by the horizon while the air turned blue with Elsie's invective.

Then, after she was finished cutting the man into tiny little pieces, she told him to bring the kid to the swim school next Monday to start lessons. On the house. Which he did.

The next summer Elsie brought me on board as a teacher at the swim school, which is still the best job I ever had. I loved teaching the kids. I lost weight from swimming all day, every day, and got the best suntan of my life, back when suntans were a fashion statement, not a cancer risk. My hair got long and sun-streaked. My pals Joel Stanner and Kerry Blanchard were also teachers, and I got to hang out with them all day. And the best part was April Merriman, a girl from my class who was also a teacher. She had this hot orange bikini, and … well, let's just say the days passed all too quickly.

Because I had a baby sister, Elsie determined that I was of the proper temperament to teach the littlest kids in the program. Because I was slightly older than most of the other teachers, she also determined that I would be well-suited to teach the adult class. And so I spent most of my days either playing in the shallow water with the toddlers or standing on the pier telling women my mother's age to ride their glides. The kids, by the way, were far easier to teach. They tended to pay attention and didn't spend the first ten minutes of each class adjusting their bathing caps.

Occasionally, I would be taken away from my duties of playing Ring-Around-the-Rosie in water that did not reach my knees, or telling women to keep moving their hands as they floated on their backs ("Out like a knife, in like a spoon, out like a knife, in like a spoon), to assist with the big kids' classes. The best of these was Lifesaving, where we teachers would play victims for the students to rescue. And we were not cooperative about it.

We'd dump entire bottles of baby oil on ourselves, and then swim out into the deep water on the outside of the pier, slippery as eels, trailing rainbow-colored slicks behind us. We'd start to "drown" and the students would swim to us—breaststroke, so as to keep their eyes on the victim at all times—and attempt to bring us in.

As soon as they tried to get an arm around us, we'd begin thrashing and fighting, sliding out of their grips, and dunking them vigorously. The kids all thought it was unfair, but the truth is, if they ever *did* have to try to haul in a panicked drowning victim, it would be that difficult, if not more. We were trying to teach them an important lesson. Also, it was fun.

The rule at the swim school was that we stayed in the water no matter how cold—and some of those mornings, we taught kids with lips the color of lapis lazuli—or how ominous the skies. When the lightning got close, we got out, but not before.

A sudden, violent thunderstorm blew in one afternoon and parked itself directly over the lake. Lightning was crashing in the trees and the wind was howling when he got the kids out of the water and under cover.

It was then that Elsie noticed a pontoon boat drifting on the other side of the lake, with a man and a dog on the deck. The man was waving his arms and yelling. She quickly dispatched Joel, Kerry, and me to go bring them in.

We got a small boat with an outboard and set out across the choppy water, Joel at the helm, and Kerry and I trying to keep the boat bailed out as the waves lapped over the sides and the rain pelted our faces. It took about ten minutes, going against the wind, to get to the pontoon, but in the storm it seemed like hours.

"Out of gas," the man said when we pulled up alongside.

We got him and his dog into the boat and set off across the lake again, riding even lower and taking on even more water. The storm was getting worse. The lightning was literally on top of us and the rain was blowing in sideways. The man didn't say a word all the way back across the lake, but the dog, a Labrador, barked constantly. I think he was actually enjoying himself.

When we got them safely on shore, the man said he was a sales representative for a big sporting goods company and would send us whatever we wanted as a token of his thanks. Kerry said he'd like some tennis balls. Joel and I chose golf balls. We never got them, by the way. But Elsie said she was proud of us and made a big fuss over us in front of all the students and parents, and that memory has lasted a lot longer than those golf balls would have.

The big event of the summer was the lake swim. All the students for the year would be invited back to the school one Saturday for a big party, which would begin with a swim all the way across Cedar Lake and back, a total distance of about a mile.

Each teacher was responsible for four or five students, and each group of students and teacher was trailed by a boat, just in case someone got too tired to finish the swim. I was lucky. I drew a bunch of twelve-year-old boys, eager to show what great swimmers they were. We raced across the lake and sat down for the mandatory half-hour waiting period before setting back out toward the swim school.

About halfway across the lake we met Elsie coming our way, poking her way through the water the way she always did.

"Slow down, boys!" she called to us. "Ride your glide!"

When the swim school season ended, I needed a job. I had decided to put off college for a year or two and earn some money. As it turned out, I'm still putting off college. The earning money part we shall skip.

At that time, the battle between Elsie and her neighbors was heating up, and Elsie drew upon my expertise as the editor of the *Lakeland High School Echo* (published weekly, except when we didn't get our stories turned in on time) to help her draft letters to Dan Luzadder, editor of *The LaGrange Standard*, defending the swim school.

One Wednesday night, while I was busily slamming together another screed on the old Royal typewriter at Elsie's house, she asked me what I would think about working for the newspaper. I said I'd probably like that.

"Good," she said, "because I talked with Dan Luzadder and told him he ought to hire you, and he said he might. You're supposed to go talk to him on Friday."

I did. I got the job. The next Monday I was working at *The LaGrange Standard* as a copy editor, sportswriter, file clerk, mailroom sorter, and cleanup boy. I made $67.50 a week and thought I was right up there with the Rockefellers. It was the first step on the road to whatever I am today. I wouldn't have taken it if Elsie hadn't been there to get me started.

I still hear from Elsie every Christmas. She left LaGrange County a few years after I worked for her, deeding the beach to the kids of LaGrange County, Indiana, and St. Joseph County, Michigan. Not that they can use it. I read in *The Standard* that after she left, someone salted the beach and swimming areas with broken glass.

Elsie's in her nineties now, living out in Washington State, where she was born and raised, and still just as sharp as ever. Up until a couple of years ago, she was still swimming, every day, in Puget Sound.

Every year I think how lucky I was that she came into my life and gave it some direction. And I know everyone else on her Christmas card list feels exactly the same way. And the further I get, the more I realize that what Elsie said was more than a swimming lesson. It was about living your life, too: Slow down; get the most out of everything you do; take your time and do it right.

Ride your glide, kids. Ride your glide.

SEVEN

You Are What You Drink

As I have—well, I was going to say matured, but that hardly seems the case. As I have gotten older, I seem to notice a blurring of the line between kidhood and adulthood. Maybe I'm wrong, but it used to seem more definite to me, when I was looking at it from the kid side of line. Kids were kids and grownups were grownups, and they lived in different worlds.

It seems different today. Kids start acting like adults at a much earlier age. And adults seem to act like kids well beyond the time when it seems appropriate or attractive.

I can't really speak to what's going on with the kids, other than to say kids have always been in too big a hurry to grow up, going back as far as anyone can remember. The difference between kids today and, say, kids in my day, the Golden Age of Kidhood, is that today's kids have a much clearer idea of what it *means* to be a grownup, or at least to look like one, and they're being aided in this cause by adults, who ought to know better. I mean, it wasn't kids who started producing and marketing thong panties for elementary school girls.

Now, to the adults who won't grow up—myself included in some respects—that is strictly a Baby Boom deal. See, there are two sides to youth culture, but in this country we only talk about the side we like—the Pepsi Generation side that tells us to be young, act young, think young. The other side is fear—fear of aging. Fear of being left out, left behind, and, ultimately, left for dead. The more we can prolong adolescence, the more we can fool ourselves into thinking that old age and death are for other people. And this is what accounts for the sales of red sports cars to people my age.

But I started, we all started, in a different time, when the kid world and the adult world were separate and by no means equal.

A kid's world was bright—all primary colors and sugar coatings, cartoons, and cereal commercials. A grownup's world was dark and mysterious, full of strange tastes and television shows where people just sat and talked.

The grownup world was, of course, intensely attractive, which shows you just how dumb we kids could be. Why we were in such a hurry to grow up is beyond me. Think about it: Grownups worried about money. All the time. The worst thing we kids had to think about was a report card. Grownups had aches and pains. All the time. We had the occasional skinned knee and once in a while, a bumped head. Grownups had bosses. We—well, P.D. and I, anyway, and later Amy—had our big sister, Vicky, who was our boss, nominally, but who did not have the power to cut off our income and force us to live in the poorhouse, which, to my kid understanding, is what bosses did.

Looking back on it, you had to be nuts to be in a hurry to grow up. Which, naturally, we all were.

Grownups didn't even eat and drink the same things as us. Martinis, for example. My Dad drank martinis and I was always curious about them. They had olives in them, which appealed to me. I loved olives. Still do. Even typing "olive" makes my mouth water.

More than that, I liked the way the word sounded—mar-TEE-nee. It seemed exotic. It conjured up images, to me anyway, of men in suits and women in high heels, talking grownup talk, playing grownup music on the hi-fi, and laughing those grownup laughs that would come drifting up the staircase when the parents had a party and you had to go to bed early. When your menu of libations is pretty much limited to juice, milk, and root beer, the very *idea* of drinking something with a name like "mar-TEE-nee" is a thrill, the good life in a stemmed glass. A "mar-TEE-nee" is *Playboy* magazine and James Bond movies and Frank Sinatra records and dancing the cha cha and eating little crackers with stinky cheese on them. It is liquid grownup.

(Actually, where the snacks are concerned, my mother had a signature party tidbit—Triscuit crackers, brushed with garlic butter and toasted in the oven. Whenever we kids saw Mom and Dad laying in a supply of Triscuits, we knew there would soon be an evening in which we were given Banquet chicken pot pies for dinner and sent to our rooms for the evening with Vicky to keep an eye on us. And we were to stay the hell out of the Triscuits. Since you always love best that which you cannot have, the Triscuit soon became my favorite cracker, a position it holds to this day.)

(My friend John Flora says being a grownup means you get to stay up all night and drink three Cokes in a row. That's good, but I would add that being a grownup also means you can eat Triscuits any time you want without your mother smacking you upside the head.)

My Dad favored a martini after work, and perhaps while watching television. For years, when he would come into our bedroom to tuck us in, I would lie there and enjoy the wonderful smell of my father's aftershave. It was ages before I realized that what I actually smelled was gin.

I was eighteen or so before I drank a martini. It was at the Holiday Inn bar in Sturgis, Michigan, a state where the legislature, in a moment of appalling stupidity, had lowered the legal drinking age to eighteen, meaning kids as young as fourteen were getting fake IDs and hitting the bars. I'm pretty sure I saw a couple of Boy Scout troops having their meetings at the Rusty Nail tavern.

I sank into one of the vinyl-covered swivel chairs in the Captain's Cove—what was it with those landlocked bars adopting nautical themes back in the 1970s, anyway? It was weird. You'd be out in the middle of the Midwest, surrounded by wheat fields as far as the eye could see. You'd walk into a hotel bar and as soon as your eyes adjusted to the subterranean level of light, you'd begin to make out the shapes of plastic crabs and nets on the wall, and over the bar you'd see the sign: Mariner's Rest, or Captain Salty's, or Ye Olde Grog Shoppe. A quick glance around the room would show your fellow mariners, most attired in the standard Midwestern uniform—baseball caps for the men, and on the women, baseball caps. They'd be looking past the giant fiberglass sailfish to the television set, which was tuned to a basketball game. Avast, me hearties, and shiver me timbers. Right.

And it was this way in bar after bar, all across the breadbasket of America, in one grain elevator town after another. All I can figure is someone, somewhere, was offering to bar owners one hell of a deal on plastic crabs. Probably the same person who is today making a killing selling them worn-out athletic equipment and tin reproductions of Wildroot hair oil signs.

Anyway, I sidled into my chair, my pals did likewise, and the waitress came over. I'm sure this was just the sort of excitement she had in mind when she took the job—serving a gang of obnoxious, blue-jeaned Indiana teenagers who had no business drinking anything stronger than Mountain Dew and who didn't yet understand the concept of the gratuity.

At the time, beer was my libation of choice. Well, check that. Funny Face drinks, the Pillsbury version of Kool-Aid, were actually my libations of choice, but I couldn't very well admit that. The days were long past when I could go up to my friends and say, "Hey, I just made a pitcher of Goofy Grape! Let's party!"

For a guy at Lakeland back then, there came a time—along about the end of your junior year, I'd say—when you were simply expected to drink beer or risk being branded as a wussy. And God help anyone who got branded as a wussy. It meant daily torment—being shut into a locker if you were small enough, being shoved into the girls' restroom if you were a bit larger, having your car tampered with in the parking lot no matter what size you were. Having no wish to visit the girls' room during the noon rush (I was *way* too big for a locker, and I had friends and cousins who could undo any car tampering I couldn't fix), I really had no choice but to go along with the crowd and drink beer. I had to, you understand. It was a matter of survival.

OK, that's a lie.

I was as eager to get started on my beer-drinking career as the next guy—not so much for the taste, or the buzz, but simply because I wasn't supposed to do it. Beer was illicit. Which, to a high school boy, is another way of saying imperative.

I can still remember my first beer (sips from your Dad's unattended bottle don't count). It was in May of my junior year. A bunch of us had gathered at a picnic grounds owned by the family of Roger Donley. It was a wonderful place—a clearing deep in the woods, overlooking a bend in Fawn River, with a big pit for bonfires and barbecues, a shelterhouse, benches and tables, and all sorts of playground equipment placed among the trees. To high school kids looking to have fun away from the prying eyes of parents or law enforcement, it was Party Central.

Someone produced beer, two cans per person. It was Budweiser. We each took our ration. As I had seen my father do a million times, I rapped the top sharply with my index finger, an exercise intended not only to reduce the chances of a beer geyser, but also to let my friends know this wasn't some neophyte they were dealing with. I was an experienced top-rapper. I knew the mechanics of beer drinking.

I pried off the pull tab, flicked it into the fire, and took a long drink. And I remember thinking quite distinctly that I really would rather have had a Coke. I ended up pouring about half of it out behind my back while the others weren't looking, and I just sort of forgot to drink the other one altogether. The plain truth was I didn't like beer.

I got over that in a hurry. By the time I was out of high school I was chugging down brews with an aplomb that would have given the old man a run for his money. And people say I didn't apply myself senior year.

So there I was, out of school and going out on the town with my pals, which meant the bar at the Holiday Inn for a warm-up drink before heading on to a roadhouse, the Matteson House, where there were rumored to be girls who didn't know us, meaning we might actually have a chance at talking to them, beyond the "Oh … hi" we usually got from females in LaGrange. The waitress took our orders—a beer for John D., a beer for Chuck, a beer for Al, a beer for Monty Jo. She got to me and for reasons I still don't understand, I said what I had heard my Dad say so many times: "mar-TEE-nee."

Her eyes widened slightly, but she said nothing. My friends looked at me funny, but didn't say anything either. A minute later she was back at the table—a beer, a beer, a beer, a beer, and my martini. She set the glass down in front of me. "Enjoy yourself, sport," she said.

I looked around the table. My friends were looking back at me. I looked at my martini—cold, clear, shimmering, its two olives impaled on one of those little plastic swords, waiting to escort me into the big leagues. With this deadly drink I was leaving behind the world of beer and Boone's Farm apple wine, which was just Kool-Aid with alcoholic content. I was about to become a bon vivant, a man about town. I was about to shed the chrysalis of my gooberish Midwestern teen exterior to show the dazzling sophisticate that I knew was buried inside. Down the hatch, boys. Next stop, the Playboy Mansion.

I took a sip.

It was vile.

It tasted like … hair tonic? Rubbing alcohol? Lighter fluid? Having never tasted any of the above, I couldn't say for sure, but it seemed to me a close approximation of what you might get if you mixed a two fingers of Vitalis with a splash of Ronsonol, and added an olive soaked with the alcohol from a thermometer at the doctor's office.

Whatever it was, it was nasty.

I don't know what I was expecting—something that tasted like olives, I suppose. I couldn't believe my tongue. And I certainly couldn't believe my father actually enjoyed these things. *Geez-o-pete*, I thought. *How am I supposed to finish this?* I had never had anything so putrid in my mouth before. I wanted to spit it into a potted plant and then go chug a bottle of Scope. The large economy size.

But finish it I did, even though every sip gave me an involuntary shudder.

This, of course, made me outrageously drunk. The feeling in my extremities went first. My feet went numb and my hands seemed not to be attached anymore. Oh, they moved, all right, but I wasn't aware of doing anything to make it happen. They just sort of drifted around, doing what hands do, lighting cigarettes, making gestures, dropping things, but they were doing it all on their own. I was just an observer.

Everything seemed to be in slow motion, like we were underwater. The room, already dark to begin with, became even more indistinct. My friends sounded like they were calling to me through a long, echoey tunnel, and as I tried to stand and walk, furniture kept jumping into my path.

I went into the parking lot, threw up, and went to sleep in the back seat of the car. When I next regained consciousness, we were leaving the Matteson House. Six hours later. I'm told I had a good time. Rumor has it I lit up the dance floor, which just goes to show you how out of my gourd I was. I do not dance.

So my first martini experience was not a good one. In fact, it was the sort of thing that a normal person would take as a clear sign: *do not do this, ever again.* Not being a normal person, however, I blew right past the warning and decided I had to keep drinking these things until I acquired a taste for them. I never was one to shrink from a challenge, including martinis, which brings up a point first raised by Indiana newspaperman Owen Hansen of the *Lebanon Reporter.* Owen opined that martini should be the plural and the singular, martinus. You have to admire someone who can combine scholarship and drinking like that.

And so, through a carefully staged plan of dedicated, long-term drinking, I got to where I enjoyed martinis. Then I got to where I enjoyed them too much. Now I haven't had a martini in about fifteen years. When I find myself in the Davey Jones' Locker, hard by the coast of Omaha, I'm usually drinking a 7-Up.

Although I think about martinis every time I put on aftershave.

Another mysterious grownup drink was coffee. Coffee, in fact, gave me entrée into the world of grownups, leading me on my first steps out of kidhood.

My mother is a coffee drinker, and not just any coffee, either. You know those coffee places, the ones on every street corner, where they have the mocha-cappuccino this and the soy-latte-frappe that? Please. To my mother, those are kiddie drinks.

Mom drinks Midwestern Farm Woman coffee, the strong stuff that walks across the kitchen, pours itself into your cup, and says, "Good morning! I'll be keeping you awake and in a high state of agitation for the next sixteen or so hours!" She does this all day, every day. Mom wears out coffee pots. She goes through about three new Mister Coffees a year.

And she's not the only one. Her entire generation of McKenzies is the same way. When we get together for family reunions, the first item of business is coffee—before the food is carried in, before the volleyball net is set up, before the chairs are arranged, before Uncle Bruce, the family secretary, takes over running the meeting from cousin John, the family president, who is smart enough not to get in Uncle Bruce's way. The coffee committee gets the coffee going, in one of those big, industrial-size coffee urns like you used to see at diners, the ones that look like locomotive boilers with a spigot on the bottom. By midmorning it is at a full rolling boil, which is then backed off to a simmer, producing a brew hot and strong enough to remove several layers of tongue and, in two cases that we know of, dissolve tonsils.

When I was a kid, my parents drank coffee made in a stovetop percolator. I have it now and use it, occasionally, because nothing smells quite like a pot of coffee bubbling away on the stove. The older I get, the more sensitive I become to things like that. The smell of a cigar brings my grandfather to life again. A fresh concord grape, with the thick, sour skin and the sweet green flesh, takes me back to the arbor at Grandma Redmond's house. And coffee bubbling on the stove—well, that was the smell of the kitchen on the mornings of my kidhood, when watching my mother make coffee was watching a ritual.

She would run the tap so the water was extra cold and extra fresh. You didn't want to make coffee with water that had been sitting in the pipes all night, you know. She'd direct that cold, fresh water into the pot, just up to the hole that led to the spout, and then place the tube and coffee basket inside. I would watch her measure out three and a third scoops of coffee, put the top on the basket and the lid on the pot, and then turn on the flame—high, but only until the moment it began to make that gurgling, burbling sound and the aroma of fresh coffee would begin wafting from the stove. Then she would turn the heat to low to keep the coffee from scorching. It was serious business, this coffee making. Or so it looked to my kid eyes.

Mom and Dad drank it black, with the little oil slicks forming on top, in mugs that were turquoise and white striped, this being the early 1960s, when everything was either turquoise and white or coral and black.

One morning I decided to make the coffee. It might have been a special occasion—Mother's Day, for instance—but I am more inclined to think it was simply a Saturday or a Sunday when I arose before everyone else, including the people at the TV station. There being nothing to watch but *The Indian Show*—known to people other than my brother and me as a test pattern—I decided to busy myself in the kitchen.

Scrambled eggs, pancakes, and biscuits were out of my league, but I had seen Mom make coffee so many times I felt pretty sure I could nail it. I drew the water into the pot, right up to the hole, just like Mom. I put in the tube and the basket and then got the yellow canister of coffee down from the cupboard.

Mom, I recalled, used three and one third scoops. Well, I reasoned, using the kid logic formed by a constant diet of commercials touting Bigger, Better, and Giant Economy Size everything, if three and third scoops is good, then six and a third scoops would be better. And so that's what I gave it.

I put the cover on the basket, spilling about a quarter-cup of grounds into the water in the process, put the lid on the percolator, and then placed it on the stove, which I cranked up to high. Soon enough it was perking merrily, which it kept doing until Mom came down, some fifteen or twenty minutes later, and turned it off.

What resulted, of course, was sludge—a thick, dark-brown-to-the-point-of-black suspension that rested, quivering, on the point between liquid and solid. It was coffee that gave you a choice—you could drink it, spoon it, or patch the roof with it. Any normal person would have thrown this stuff away, but parents are not normal people. And so my mother poured a cup—well, plopped it into a cup would probably be a better description—and pronounced it good coffee.

That was all it took. From then on I appointed myself weekend coffee maker. I made it my duty to get up before everyone else every Saturday and Sunday so I could make a pot of that good coffee for my folks. Although after a couple of weeks of that, I noticed that no matter how early I got up, my Mom was up before me and the coffee was already made. Go figure. And on the mornings when I did beat her to the kitchen, she usually managed to intercept me in time to get me to scale back on the strength, just a bit. In a few months, I was actually making a pretty decent (that is, drinkable) pot of coffee.

Now, just because I was making coffee didn't mean I got to taste it. Rhode Islanders, I understand, start their children on a concoction called coffee milk—milk with sweetened coffee syrup. No such shenanigans at our house. Coffee was forbidden to children until Mom said you were old enough, which varied by child. My older sister Vicky, for example, a responsible child who always minded her manners, picked up after herself, and did as she was told, qualified for coffee at age twelve, although she didn't drink it then. This made no sense to me. It was like having a driver's license but no interest in driving a car.

My brother P.D. and I were not like Vicky, and so we didn't qualify to drink coffee until … well, let me think. I was in high school. In fact, it was in high school that I developed a taste for hot water coffee. To make hot water coffee, you get a cup down from the shelf, spoon into it a generous amount of freeze-dried coffee crystals, fill the cup with hot water from the tap, and enjoy. Well, "enjoy" may be too strong a word. Let's just keep it at "drink," because truth be told, hot water coffee is pretty godawful. However, it is the only way you can recreate at home the taste of coffee from a highway rest area vending machine. It is also the fastest cup of coffee you can make, which is important when the school bus arrives at 6:20 A.M. and you get up at 6:10. More than once, I ran out the door with a Dixie cup of hot water coffee in one hand and a handful of dry cereal in the other. This, plus a couple of cigarettes sneaked out in the parking lot before class began, was my breakfast of champions.

So I was in high school when Mom finally decided I was mature enough to drink coffee. As for my brother—well, I'm not sure P.D. has permission yet. And the baby of the family, my sister Amy, never had any interest in it, which, of course, has given rise on more than one occasion to the theory that she may have been adopted.

Now, because parents don't want their children to be able to figure them out—ever—their rules are riddled with inconsistencies. For example, while coffee was out of the question until you reached the age of Mom Says It's OK, it was perfectly permissible for us to drink hot tea. Try to figure that one out. I never could, although Mom and I had several deep and wide-ranging discussions on the matter:

Mike: How come I can drink tea but I can't have coffee?

Mom: Shut up or you won't be drinking tea, either.

Of course, this was but one of many Mom Contradictions which served to make our daily lives so … well, I was going to say interesting, but the better word is probably confusing. You never knew what the rule was from day to day, which I think was the point. As long as Mom could keep us off-balance, she had a chance of maintaining some control.

Some examples:

"Pick up your feet!" followed by "Must you stomp around like that?"

"Clean your plate!" followed by "Your butt's not getting any smaller," which was often paired with, "Don't bolt your food!" followed by "Would you please stop dawdling?"

"Go outside! I'm tired of having you underfoot all day long!" followed by "Why are you never around when I need you?"

And, of course, the ever-popular:

"Close the door, were you born in a barn?" followed by "If you slam that door one more time …"

As for that one about being born in a barn—ever popular in LaGrange County, of course, where some of us may have indeed been born in barns—a friend of mine once responded, "Yes. My father was a jackass and my mother was an old nag." That was 1970, and as far as I know, she's still grounded.

OK, back to tea. Now, what I drank in those days was tea only in the technical sense. I had rather a heavy hand with the sugar bowl back then—a bowl of Cheerios wasn't palatable to me without at least a quarter-cup of sugar on it—and I approached tea with this same generous touch. Really, I was drinking simple syrup, sugar and water, with a teaspoon of Nestea instant tea thrown in for color.

But I thought I was very big stuff, indeed, sitting there at the kitchen table on a winter afternoon after school, the young lord of the manor sipping his tea and poring over his homework. Not that the tea made me any smarter. There's a Japanese proverb that says, "If man has no tea in him, he is incapable of understanding truth and beauty." Maybe. However, I can report that in my case, a boy *with* tea in him still doesn't have much chance of understanding how to diagram a sentence.

It's interesting to me that I have come full-circle. The tea-drinking boy eventually became a young man whose main sources of liquid refreshment were coffee in the mornings (as many as twelve cups a day, when I worked the early shift at *The Indianapolis News* and had to be at my desk by 4:30 A.M.) and booze at night—beer mostly, but also scotch and Irish whisky, and, of course, those martinis I mentioned.

The booze went by the wayside first. I reached a point in my life where I realized I liked it too much. I had to control it before it controlled me. My father had struggled with alcohol, and I didn't want to have to fight the same fight. I remembered watching, appalled, as my father opened a can of beer, drank off the first two swallows, and then poured vodka into the can to top it off. When I found myself doing the same thing, I knew it was time to stop. And so I did.

Then my physician, Dr. Shecky, the world's funniest (he thinks) family physician, trying to get my blood pressure down to manageable numbers, took me off coffee. At first I switched to decaf, where I followed the advice of friends and bought the strongest decaf I could find. That way, they said, you can fool yourself into thinking you're drinking real coffee.

All I could think of was that it looked an awful lot like the coffee I used to make for my parents.

After a year or so of decaf, with my pressure under control again, I began drinking tea. I tried decaf tea, but it was a waste of time. There seems to be no decaf tea that tastes like—well, like anything. It's like drinking hot water. And so I started drinking regular tea, and that is now my morning beverage—a nice cup or two of Darjeeling, plain, no sugar. And in the evenings, I drink nothing stronger than ginger ale.

In other words, I'm drinking pretty much the same stuff I drank in kidhood. I'd probably be drinking Funny Face now if they still made it. It's sad to think I may never again know the artificial flavor and color of Goofy Grape, Lefty Lemon, and, my personal favorite, Loudmouth Lime.

I have come full circle, on beverages anyway. Without any conscious effort on my part I seem to have learned, somewhere along the line, that being a grownup has nothing to do with alcohol and coffee. It isn't what you drink that makes you an adult after all, anymore than it is what you wear or what you drive. It is your ability to diagram sentences. Which I still cannot do.

EIGHT

Love in the Time of Mononucleosis

It was taken as a matter of faith among many Lakeland High School boys (those of us who did not have steady girlfriends, mostly, and even some of us who did) that the girls in the next towns down the road—in our case, Kendallville to the south; Sturgis, Michigan, to the north; Goshen to the west; and Angola to the east—were different from the girls with whom we went to school. By virtue of geography (the only context in which the word "virtue" would be appropriate for us) they were prettier, sexier, better built, and more … *agreeable.* And it was that last one that mattered most. When you are a sixteen- or seventeen- or eighteen-year-old guy whose hormones have recently become so active as to be carbonated, the idea that somewhere close by, a twenty- or thirty-minute drive away, there might be a girl who is agreeable … well, it's the sort of thing that keeps your hopes alive.

And what were we hoping for? Use your imagination. We did.

We had to. Sex, for us, was mostly theoretical. We had heard of it, we had reason to believe it existed, we hoped to put some of our theories into practice someday, but we were dismally short on actual experience. Most of us knew only what could be gained from looking at *Playboy* magazine, listening to the older guys, and participating in a few feverish make-out sessions in the front seats of our parents' cars, parked late at night in the darker and more remote corners of the Pigeon River Fish and Wildlife Area.

Which is to say, not much.

Parking was actually nothing more than a teenager's game of hide-and-seek. An amorous couple would drive onto the dirt roads along the Pigeon River, poking their way further and further onto what we called "The State Ground"—old farms that had been reclaimed by the state as a habitat for pheasant, deer, and wood ticks. The lovebirds would retreat into the wilderness—well, as close as we got to wilderness, anyway—until they found a place they thought secluded from prying eyes, where they could Do What Comes

Naturally. Or so they hoped.

Those of us who were *sans amour* would go looking for them, an exercise we called "bushwhacking." I saw "we" because two of the more successful bush-whackers of that era were Monty Jo Strawser and myself.

Our combined talents lent themselves perfectly to the enterprise. We had near-encyclopedic knowledge of the territory, seeing as how we grew up next to it. It was, literally, our backyard (my grandmother's birthplace, on a wide bend in the river, was among those farms the state had reclaimed). We also had terrific night vision, which enabled us to drive for long stretches on dark, narrow country roads with the headlights off. And, since we didn't have girlfriends, we had plenty of time. Looking back, I can't see how we could have become anything but first-class bushwhackers.

A typical hunt went something like this: We would spend the evening in La-Grange, doing what all kids in LaGrange did back then—driving in a circuit we called "The Tool," as in "we're tooling town." Don't ask me where it came from. In other towns it was called "cruising" or "chopping" or "driving around aim-lessly yelling at each other," but in LaGrange it was tooling.

The loop went around the courthouse square, and then south on Detroit Street, the main drag through town, pausing if necessary at what was then the county's only honest-to-goodness, red-yellow-and-green stop light. You'd con-tinue south on Detroit Street to the A&W, whip into their lot, and then back out again to go back north on Detroit Street, through the stoplight and to the courthouse, where you'd start all over again.

And you would do this by the hour, occasionally stopping in at the Dairy Queen for a coke or the A&W for a root beer. The Dairy Queen was a sit-down place and the A&W had carhops. Monty Jo and I chose the Dairy Queen, hav-ing been Banned For Life from the A&W after an episode in which we drove to Sturgis, bought a large bucket of Kentucky Fried Chicken, took it back to the A&W, ordered small root beers, ate the chicken, and threw the bones out the window into the parking lot. The owners of the A&W took this as conclusive proof that we were on drugs. We were directed to take our business elsewhere or be turned over to The Authorities. For what, I am not sure. Littering, I sup-pose. Or being high on the Colonel's secret recipe of eleven herbs and spices.

Anyway, after a brief pause for refreshment we would pile back into the car and rejoin the parade of cars rolling up and down Detroit Street.

I've often wondered if we drove in circles because we simply weren't clever enough to think of other ways to occupy ourselves, or if it was because we were teenaged kids in a small town with few options where entertainment was concerned. A teenaged kid in a small town is like a caged animal, full of restless energy that has to find some sort of release. Perhaps we were like captured tigers stalking back and forth in their cages, or polar bears swimming endless laps in their pool at the zoo.

No.

We weren't clever enough to think of other ways to occupy ourselves.

As we drove, Monty Jo and I and our friends—bushwhacking is *always* a group endeavor—would take note of which couples we had seen on the tool: Boyfriend at the wheel, girl sitting in the center of the front seat, right next to him, so as to prove to one and all the depths of their love, until her parents came downtown for an ice cream cone and she quickly scooted back over toward the passenger door.

We would also note which couples we had *not* seen in the last ten or twelve times around the circuit. Odds were they had gone parking. Our quarry identified, we would head out to the State Ground and loose the hounds. Which is to say, us.

The trick to successful bushwhacking is stealth. Driving without headlights, as I mentioned, was critical. So was knowing exactly how far your car would coast, given its speed and the lay of the land. Let's say your quarry was parked back along the river near Nasby's Dam. You had to time it so that you could turn off your engine and roll stealthily down the road and into the parking area until the car was right behind your quarry's Lovemobile. Then, you would start the engine, honk the horn, and hit the lights (high beams). If it was someone you knew well, you might even get out of the car with flashlights (we always carried flashlights under the front seats for just such emergencies) and run up to shine them in the windows.

What did we see? Not much. Oh, there were tales of couples caught in a complete state of nakedidity, shame on them, but I cannot say I ever saw anything approaching that level of dishabille. I remember the hilarity of seeing tousled heads popping up and whipping around in the glare of the headlights, and occasionally you might see a girl hurriedly smoothing out her clothes and glaring at her boyfriend for getting her into such a fine mess, but that's about it.

In fact, as I think about it today, it is the glare that comes back to haunt me. I can't recall that we ever once took into consideration the feelings of a girl who might be caught in a compromising situation. All we wanted to do was embarrass the couple, especially the guy. We were pigs. Or, considering our tender years, piglets. To think about about how a girl might have felt being caught in a compromising position would have required a sensitivity we did not possess, of which we were not yet capable. I, myself, was still at least a decade away from such enlightenment. OK, two decades.

So no doubt you are thinking that all this bushwhacking was a sign of jealousy. Am I right? You're thinking that Monty Jo and I and our fellow bushwhackers would have given our eye teeth to trade places with the bushwhackees, to be the guy engaged in the liplock, fogging up the windows of his dad's Buick.

Well, *of course* we were. But we were inept with girls. Oh, we could be friends with them and we occasionally had dates, usually with girls one or two years younger than us in the time-honored high school tradition of Underclass Girl Poaching.

But True Life Teen Romance, with the pledges of eternal love and the ceremonial trading of class rings and all that goes with it, or more accurately all we *presumed* goes with it, was another matter entirely.

And so we lived rich and vivid fantasy lives, in which the girls from the next town, the *agreeable* girls, didn't slap us or shriek when our hands wandered a little too close to the Forbidden Zones, didn't throw us over for older guys, didn't laugh in our faces when we asked if maybe they'd sort of like to maybe sort of see a movie or something sometime, maybe. The girls from the next town said "yes."

Of course, like many matters of faith, the belief that the girls in the next town were different was completely untrue. And like many matters of faith, the possibility of something that may or may not be wonderful, just out of our reach, blinded us to the things that were truly wonderful right in our midst. Or, to put it simply, Cindy Crawford could have been the junior class vice president and we still would have insisted there were prettier girls in Kendallville. We were morons. Then again, since I've already established that we were piglets, and given the fact that we were high school boys and, by definition, morons, I guess that goes without saying.

Probably the worst example of my own swinishness came about at the prom of my senior year. To this day, I don't know what came over me. Wait. Yes, I do. Hormones and booze and stupidity came over me. And I still feel a slight blush of embarrassment, all these years later, over what transpired …

It is my senior year at Lakeland and I am caught in that strange vortex of wanting to get the hell out and see what the world has to offer, and at the same time wanting to make sure I have gotten everything I could out of the High School Experience. If high school is a lemon—and for me, it was—then at least I should make sure I have squeezed every last drop of juice from it before I throw the rind on the compost heap that has been my life so far. Or something.

At any rate, as we leave winter and wheel into the spring of 1972, the one thing I have not experienced in my three years at high school has been The Fabled Senior Prom.

Up until now, I have been convinced that the prom is, in fact, a crock. I am vociferously anti-pretense, and a prom is *nothing* but pretend. I don't care how many tons of crepe paper you hang from the rafters, or how many thousands of balloons you inflate, you cannot turn a high school gymnasium into something it is not: A riverboat or an oriental garden or an antebellum southern mansion (those being the only three themes ever considered by Prom Committees). All it takes is one person opening the door, one sudden change in the air pressure causing a whoosh of air from the locker rooms and out from under the bleachers, and the Good Ship Magnolia Blossom or whatever theme those moony-eyed girls on the decoration committee came up with will be transformed back into what it really is, a gym, with its signature aroma of old sweat socks and stale popcorn.

By the same token, you can't squeeze pimply seniors into tuxedoes or giggling juniors into ball gowns and expect them to turn into Clark Gables and Vivian Leighs. There are not many sixteen-, seventeen-, and eighteen-year-old bon vivants and sophisticates anywhere in the world, much less in places like LaGrange, where they still have a hitching rail for horse-drawn buggies on the west side of the courthouse.

The prom, I tell myself, is bogus. This belief is in keeping with my role as the senior class's leading iconoclast. That's what I call myself, anyway. Teachers and administrators have other names for the kind of kid I am, "disruptive influence" and "smartass" being the two with which I am most familiar.

Lakeland is just like any other school, or any other society for that matter: From the moment you arrive, you go into a group. Either you are shoehorned into it, or you shoehorn yourself into it. And that is how you are known until you break out and make your own way.

When I first get to Lakeland, I am a music geek—band and choir both, and swing choir to boot—and an A-minus, B-plus student (well, and that C in geometry). I never challenge authority, never swim against the tide. I defer to upperclassmen, do my homework, join clubs, take part in activities, smile at the teachers. I am a Nice Kid.

Midway through my junior year, something snaps. School gets boring and I am not having any fun. I need a new group. I don't want to be a Nice Kid any more.

Being a jock is out. My father wants me to be a jock. No way am I going to do that. Besides, jocks are identified, and cast in their roles, as early as seventh grade. I would be too late to get in on the jock deal even if I *didn't* have dad issues.

I can't be a brain, either. At the time I started losing interest in school, those A-minus, B-plus grades of mine began traveling south. At this point in my career, they were somewhere around Macon, Georgia, and showing no sign of reversing their direction. What's more, being a brain takes work, and I have already worked and found it not to my liking.

I hang on to some of my music geek status, although I bail on swing choir, which is unheard of. Swing choir is the elite, the top drawer, the cream of the crop, and I got in as a sophomore, which is rare indeed. But I decide to quit anyway. Swing choir seems dopey to me now. I prefer stage band, which plays what we think is jazz, and marching band, because I am the drum major and get to lord it over everyone.

What I like best is journalism class. It is full of smart alecks who drink coffee and smoke cigarettes and offer withering put-downs of just about everything—other people, other activities, and especially school traditions. Journalism class is the Lakeland High School distribution center for iconoclasts. So that is what I become.

But there's a problem. Now I am an iconoclast who, for reasons I do not fully comprehend, wants to go to the Prom. I want to belong. I want to take a magical ride on the Good Ship Magnolia Blossom. That's not the problem.

The problem is I must first overcome some obstacles, such as not having a girlfriend.

This is actually a fairly easy hurdle to clear. At Lakeland there exists a wide-ranging and powerful Girl Network, the members of which take very seriously one another's academic, physical, and social well-being. A hint ("I was thinking about going to the prom") dropped to a member of the Girl Network just before the start of first period results in a report back by lunchtime: "Phyllis wants to go to the prom," it says. "She would probably go with you."

Phyllis is Phyllis Cain, a girl I know from band and a few extracurricular activities. She's nice. Cute. Sweet. I've always liked Phyllis and I think she likes me OK. She never said she didn't, which is pretty good for me. I decide to ask her.

At the end of the school day I seek out Phyllis in the senior hall.

"Hi," I say.

"Hi," says Phyllis, who, despite already being briefed by the Girl Network, pretends she doesn't know what's coming, that this is just another conversation with a classmate.

"So, um, Phyllis. Phyll. Heh heh. Um. You going to the prom?"

"Oh, I don't know. Are you?"

"Well, I wasn't going to, but I kind of thought this being senior year and all …"

"Yes, I know. Senior year."

"So I was kinda thinking it might be kinda fun to sort of go. You know. Sort of a fling."

"Yes, it might."

"And I was kinda wondering if, well, you know, if you didn't have anyone else to go with, you know, maybe we could kinda go together."

"That might be nice."

"I mean, we wouldn't have to be like boyfriend and girlfriend or anything …"

"No, no …"

"Just a couple of pals going to the prom to see what it's like because we're seniors and we'll never have this chance again …"

"Right. Absolutely."

"Just for fun."

"Yes. Fun."

"So."

"So."

"You, um, wanna go with me?"

"I'll get back to you."

The next day the executive committee of the Girl Network confers and approves me, six votes to five with one abstention (Phyllis, I think). I get the news as I am finishing lunch. I have a prom date.

My next hurdle—convincing Mom to give me the money I'll need—also goes smoother than expected. I am broke, and if I am going to do this right I will need Mom's largesse, which she bestows with only a short version of her standard lecture, "You Kids Must Think I Am Made Out Of Money." She hardly flinches when I tell her I'll need dough for a tuxedo, some spending money to boot, and the unlimited use of the nicer of our two Fords come prom night. Then she throws me a curve.

"What about flowers?" she says.

"Huh?"

"A corsage, dimwit," offers my big sister Vicky, home from college, where she has acquired what she thinks is a veneer of sophistication. Every few weeks she brings it home from Terre Haute—you know, the big town—to swan around for her rube siblings. She is smirking at the thought of me dressing up and trying to behave like an adult.

"Oh, yeah. I knew that," I say, lying.

"Well, make sure to get nice ones," says Mom, thinking, perhaps, of the corsages she never got. "And pick out a decent tuxedo. Don't embarrass me. Nothing garish." My mother knows me too well.

OK, so now I have the date and I have the bankroll. All that remains is for me to tell Monty Jo and my scoffing pals, the manly men with whom I have scorned proms past.

Rather than just coming out and saying it, I decide to play it cool and offer information only if asked. I am counting on the fact that of all the questions Monty Jo Strawser is likely to ask me, "Are you going to the prom?" will probably not be among them.

About three weeks before prom time, I drive up to the men's store in Sturgis to see about renting a tuxedo. The guy at the store hates prom season and the endless parade of adolescent goofballs it brings to his store. You can tell by the way he lifts the sample book out from behind the case and heaves it onto the counter. It has barely landed—*thump*—when he starts walking away.

"There you go," he says over his shoulder as he heads off toward some neckties that need straightening. "Look through the book and see if there's anything you want. I'll be over here."

I begin leafing through the heavy, laminated pages. Because this is the early 1970s, I am presented with photo after photo of the more eye-popping examples of men's formalwear, crushed-velvet numbers in vivid shades of orange and green and blue, with lapels as wide as car doors and pants flared enough on the bottom to hide a medium-sized dog. The shirts are just as showy, with ruffles cascading down the front in a manner befitting your average conga musician. And the ties? My God. The ties are huge, hideous things, giant luna moths made of satin in the same vivid shades as the suits. They'd qualify as clown ties, except that your average clown has better taste than to wear such a monstrosity. Which means I am instantly drawn to them.

I have just about settled on a single-breasted baby blue number with dark blue trim and rounded lapels about fourteen inches across—The Moonglow, it says in the catalog—when something holds me up. I wish it could say it was my innate good taste asserting itself, but I really think it was my Anabaptist roots, Mennonite ancestors on Grandma's side, those conservative pioneers who came to Indiana from Switzerland with nothing more than a dream of religious freedom and a box of dessert recipes, clucking their tongues fiercely at me from beyond and channeling their displeasure into a tape loop of my mother's voice: "Pick out a decent tuxedo … pick out a decent tuxedo … pick out a decent tuxedo … *nothing garish garish garish …*"

I turn the page away from the temptation of shocking blue crushed velvet and settle instead on a black tuxedo. Plain. Sensible. Classic. Nothing garish for me, thanks. No, sir, I'll just stick with the basics.

I choose a Mennonite tuxedo. And we aren't even Mennonites.

However, my devil-may-care side asserts itself when it comes to haberdashery, and I do go with a ruffled shirt. You only live once, after all.

The salesman is looking out the window, smoking a Pall Mall. "Excuse me," I say. "I've made up my mind."

"OK," says the salesman, stubbing out his cigarette. "Which one? Oh, that. The Stork Club. Huh. I woulda figured you for a Moonglow. Size?"

"I dunno."

He sighs. "Just stand normal," he says, whipping his tape measure around me, including those places where, at that point in my life, I was *really* not comfortable with the idea of being measured.

"Forty-two long," he says, jotting some numbers down on a pad. "You need accessories? Cufflinks? Cummerbund? Don't ask for a top hat because we aren't renting top hats anymore. They kept coming back full of barf." Well, I think, there goes *that* idea.

"Lakeland Prom? That's the twentieth. The suit will be here the eighteenth. Gotta have it back by Monday the twenty-second."

And he walks away. Just like that. No, "Thanks for stopping in." No, "See you in a couple of weeks." No, "How are you fixed for socks and underwear?" He just goes back to the window and fires up another Pall Mall.

I leave the store and drive home, where Monty Jo is waiting for me in the back yard.

"Where ya been, Mikey?" he asks, grinning.

"Sturgis."

"Whatcha go to Sturgis for?" The grin is getting bigger.

"Just lookin' around."

"That's not what I heard," he says. "I heard you were up there renting a monkey suit so you could take someone to the prom. Lah-de-dah."

I have been ratted out. And to make matters worse, the rat who ratted me, the one stepping out from behind Monty Jo, is none other than my sweet baby sister, Amy, age five. If it had been Vicky or P.D. I might have contemplated some retaliatory action, but not Amy. Never Amy.

"Hi, Mikey!" she says. "I told Monty Jo you were gettin' a zeedo."

"Tuxedo."

"Is it in the car? Can I see it?"

"Yeah, Mikey," says Monty Jo. "Can we see it? Oh please, Mikey! Pretty please?" He is cracking himself up.

"No," I say. "It won't be ready for a couple of weeks."

"Darn!" says Amy.

"Yeah, darn!" says Monty Jo. He is enjoying himself way too much, if you ask me.

I walk into the house, blushing furiously. Monty Jo and Amy follow.

"So who ya takin' to the prom, Mikey?" he asks. "Huh? Huh? Who ya takin' to the prom?"

Before I can answer, my big sister's voice calls out from the living room: "Phyllis Cain!"

And then Monty Jo does something I do not expect. He smiles. Genuinely.

"Hey, that's good," he says. "I like Phyllis. She's nice. You guys will have fun." He turns to greet my mother as she walks into the kitchen. "Mom!" he yells. "What's for dinner? Amy invited me."

It is another in the long list of times when I cannot figure out my best friend. I just know he is my best friend for a very good reason.

The next three weeks pass without event, save for a couple of times when members of the Girl Network—some of those who voted against me, I think—check to make sure I'm still planning to take Phyllis to the prom. Since these girls carhop at the A&W, my guess is that they think they need to keep a close eye on a drug-addled chicken-bone tosser such as myself.

The day of the prom, I drive to Sturgis to pick up my suit and the corsage. The suit looks to be as advertised—a plain black tuxedo. The corsage is nice, not so showy as to be lurid but not so understated as to make me look like a piker. So far, so good. I take the tux home, hang the suit in my closet, stash the flowers in the icebox, and then set about washing and waxing the car.

The car done, and parked away from the trees so it doesn't get bombed by the flock of particularly incontinent birds who have moved in this year, I shower and shave and begin to dress. Surprise of surprises, the tuxedo fits. I don't know why I thought it wouldn't, but for some reason I had fretted all day about the pants being too tight or the sleeves being too short, but they're not. It actually fits.

I check myself in the mirror. Not bad, I think. "Vestis virum reddit," recalling my ninth-grade Latin. "Clothes make the man."

Until I look down, that is, and see that the shoes I am wearing are scuffed. Did I say scuffed? I mean, the shoes that I am wearing look like someone held them to a grinding wheel.

For a moment I think about trying to pass them off as two-tone, black and gray, but even I recognize how dopey that sounds. So off comes the jacket, the pants, the tie, the shirt, and downstairs I go in my underwear to look for the shoeshine kit. I finally find it, buried under a pile of gloves and stocking hats, in the hall closet. I haul it upstairs and set to work trying to rehabilitate my shoes.

I slather on a thick coat of Kiwi, brush it out, and buff it. Now the shoes are acceptable. My hands, however, are not. They look like I have been mining coal. Back into the bathroom I go, where I use up most of a cake of Lava and wear the bristles off a nail brush trying to get rid of all that black gunk. When I emerge, I have two little red claws where my hands used to be. But they're clean.

I climb back into the monkey suit, giving it one last look in the mirror, using my red (but clean) pincers to adjust my pocket square as I imagine Cary Grant might have done, were his pocket square the kind that comes with my tuxedo, a little triangle of fabric stapled to a cardboard card. I go downstairs, present myself to my snickering family—snickering except for Amy, who thinks I look beautiful—and head out the door to the car.

Phyllis lives about four miles from our house. I have traveled three of those four miles when I remember her corsage is still in the refrigerator at home, on the second shelf, right next to a pound of Lebanon bologna and half a roll of braunschweiger.

I turn around and go back. My mother is standing in the driveway with the corsage box in her hand. "Took you long enough," she says. Vicky stands next to her, laughing uproariously. I whip the car back out into the road and take off with a screech of rubber and a shower of gravel.

Finally, I get to Phyllis's house. I ring the bell. She answers. She looks very pretty. Her hair is done up nice, and her dress is a long, flowing, empire-waisted thing. Her folks take pictures of us with an Instamatic. Blinking from the blasts of the flash cube, I give Phyllis her corsage while she pins a white carnation to my sensible black Mennonite lapel.

We drive to school, me at the wheel, Phyllis sitting over by the door. We're just pals, after all.

The prom at Lakeland is a production of the junior class. It is their gift to the departing seniors—a night of dazzling romance before the upperclassmen go off into the cold, cruel world. Well, as much dazzling romance as you can fake with crepe paper and balloons in a stinky gymnasium, anyway.

As we enter the gym, catching that faint whiff of sweatsocks from the boys' locker room just off the main doors, a member of the junior class asks us our names.

"What?" I say. This might be a good time to point out that the guy doing the asking has known me for years. He knows my name as well as he knows his own. I stare at him.

"You gotta tell me your names so I can announce you," he says.

"OK, I'm Yukon Moose Cholak and this is Joanie Weston of the San Francisco Bay Area Bombers," I say, citing the names of my favorite professional wrestler and Roller Derby queen.

"Miss Phyllis Cain and Mr. Mike Redmond," the humorless twerp bellows into a microphone.

The next few hours are a blur of girls rushing up to each other, squealing, and whispering in each others' ears while the guys give each other high-fives and tell dirty jokes, as teachers and their spouses circulate among us. In other words, it is just another school dance, only better-dressed.

We get our pictures taken. We graze on sandwiches, cookies, and punch. We make a few half-hearted stabs at dancing. I say half-hearted because the music for the evening apparently was chosen with our chaperones in mind. It amounts to one-third of a polka band—drums, bass, accordion, and trumpet—and goes by the name Mello-tones or Marvel-aires or some such. We are told they've brought their distinctive musical stylings all the way from Elkhart. You know, Music City.

The music seems to be an endless version of "Satin Doll". It is not rock and roll, that's for sure. It isn't even polka. The teachers seem to love it, which ought to tell you everything you need to know about how we kids reacted. It was like being trapped in an episode of the *Lawrence Welk Show*.

At about the nine o'clock hour we are herded into the auditorium for some more entertainment—a stage hypnotist who dragoons about ten kids into being part of his act. One of those is my cousin John, who is given the hypnotic suggestion that he is four years old. It is excruciating to watch my big, hulking cousin up there jabbering away in baby talk, but I force myself, knowing that it could come in handy someday should I need a little leverage in a negotiation. John won't remember and I'll probably be able to convince him he peed his pants up there.

Then we troop back into the gym for the crowning of the king and queen—Dennis Spreuer and Jeanne Woodworth, no surprise there. They've won more Cute Couple awards than any other twosome in the history of Lakeland High School. They get their pictures taken with Imperial Margarine crowns on their heads.

And then comes the promenade. No kidding. They really make us do that. We line up four abreast, girls resting their hands in the crooks of their escorts' arms, and walk in a big circle around the gym while parents, watching from the mezzanine, take photos with more of those Instamatics and those silly flash cubes.

And then it is over. The Good Ship Magnolia Blossom has pulled into port and tied up. The crepe paper is drooping, the balloons are deflating. Collars are coming open, bow ties are lost. Hair is coming undone and stiff, crinkly evening gowns are beginning to wilt.

It is now time for us to begin doing what we had been waiting to do all night: Go out and drink.

By pre-arrangement, a bunch of us have planned to gather at Mike Pipher's house in LaGrange, his parents being out of town. And so, after a few laps of tooling in our evening clothes, several carloads of us peel off the main drag and drive up to the Pipher's big, old house. Mike's older brother Jack is already there. Jack, who is my sister Vicky's age and therefore a man of the world, has appointed himself bartender and chaperone. His job is to keep the drinks as weak as possible and keep us off the streets until morning.

Now, among the happy, well-dressed couples convening at the Pipher residence this evening are my classmate Bud Axley and a girl I do not know. What I *do* know is that she is pretty. Very pretty. Her name is Denise. And she does not go to Lakeland.

Bud has brought a girl from the next town down the road.

For the next couple of hours, all goes well. After changing back into civilian clothes, we sit around the Piphers' comfortable living room chatting amiably, sipping whiskey sours and sloe gin fizzes, our idea of sophisticated drinks, which Jack has mixed so as to have only slightly more kick than Kool-Aid.

By some circumstance, I find myself alone in the living room with Denise. Bud and Phyllis are out in the kitchen. Some other kids are in the parlor. A few are outside. And Denise and I begin making out—tentatively, at first, just smooches, really. And then things become a little more heated. Fog up the windows on Dad's Buick? Ha. We are fogging up the windows on the Piphers' second floor.

Which is when Bud comes into the room to check on his date.

"Hi, Buddy!" she says. And then we go back to kissing. Denise, in addition to being very pretty, is a first-class kisser, and I like to think I am holding my own in the osculation department as well. This is the most fun I've had since that hypnotist made Larry Greenawalt crow like a chicken.

Bud is furious, as he has a right to be. He storms around the room, gathering up glasses and ashtrays and muttering darkly. If it had been me, I would have told me to step outside, but Bud isn't the step-outside kind of guy. He's the storm-around-gathering-glasses-and-ashtrays-and-mutter kind of guy. We continue to kiss. Jack comes in the room. We continue to kiss. Half the senior class of Lakeland High School comes through the room. We continue to kiss.

Buddy, finally, has had enough. "We have to go," he informs Denise.

"Keep your shirt on," she says.

And then two things happen: Phyllis comes into the room, and that tape loop in my head starts back up again. This time my mother's voice is saying "Don't embarrass me … Don't embarrass me … Don't embarrass me." And I am, of course, deeply embarrassed. I am a dog. A dirty, no-good dog. No, I'm worse than that. I have abandoned my date and hooked up with someone else's girl—at the prom! The night of magic and romance! I might as well have floated a turd in the punchbowl while I was at it.

I am a pig.

Bud and Denise leave. Phyllis, God bless her, comes into the room and sits down next to me as if nothing had happened. She's a good girl who didn't deserve to be saddled with a clod like me for a prom date. I feel rotten to the core.

The sun is just beginning to come up as I pull into Phyllis's driveway. I walk her to her door. Her corsage is wilted. My carnation disappeared hours ago. We look like two people who have been up way past their bedtimes. Like about two days past their bedtimes.

"I had a really nice time," she says. "Thank you."

And then she kisses me and goes inside.

Prom night is over.

I wish I could say I realized at that moment the true meaning of agreeable, the kind of agreeable that counts. I wish I could say that Phyllis's equanimity taught me an important lesson about learning to roll with the punches and look on the bright side, to forgive people when they do stupid things and just keep pushing forward with your life. But I can't. I went home, threw up in the driveway, slept all day and spent the better part of the next two weeks trying to get up the nerve to track down Denise. Which I never did. I never saw her again. Although I have thought about her a lot, over the years. She really was that pretty. And a good kisser.

But over the years I have seen Phyllis at class reunions, and she strikes me as the same good girl she always was. It's always nice to see her, even if I do still get a twinge of guilt about prom night.

Oh, and where girls from other towns were concerned: A few weeks after the prom, a guy named Jerry told Monty Jo and me that he was going down to Kendallville to see this hot little number he knew down there. He was regaling us with his plans for all the hot-cha-cha he anticipated would be part of the evening's festivities, including a side trip out to Pigeon River, if you know what I mean.

I asked her name. He told me. It was my cousin.

I told my mom, who told her mom, and from the way Jerry acted the next time I saw him, I am pretty sure she sat next to the passenger door all night long. I know for sure Monty Jo and I didn't see him that night when we were out bushwhacking.

NINE

Naked Lady Mudflaps

(with Footnotes!)[1]

Men and women are different. I don't know why this continues to astonish people, but it does. In fact, every sitcom on television is based on this premise: Men and women are different, and it's astonishing. Hilarity ensues. But it isn't astonishing, not in the least.

I happen to think being different is a good thing, and not only for the obvious reasons. I enjoy the company of my manly men friends, with whom I get together to do manly man things (ride motorcycles, belch, and trade recipes), but when I need a change of pace, I choose to be with a woman (same stuff, without the belching). And if a woman isn't available, I hang out with my dog (same stuff, without the motorcycles or recipes).

For years, some well-meaning but misguided people tried to convince us that save for a few exterior modifications, men and women were essentially the same beings. This is simply not true. Isn't it obvious? Men can't have babies, and women can't write their names in the snow. We're not built the same and more importantly, we're not wired the same. There may be some men who long to know what it's like to birth a baby, but I have yet to meet a woman who thinks it would be cool to pee her initials into a snowbank. See? Different. And the sooner we accept that, the happier we'll all be.

Take the title of this chapter: Naked Lady Mudflaps. Every guy I know likes Naked Lady Mudflaps—you know, the ones you see on the backs of semis, and some of the larger models of pickup truck as well, with the shiny chrome silhouette of a woman (I, personally, think she's a redhead) exhibiting what we may call bounteous proportions. Oh, we may say they're stupid. We may say they objectify women. We may say they're in questionable taste. We might even

---

[1] Like this!

mean it. Even so, it doesn't matter. We may not admit it, but guys like Naked Lady Mudflaps.

Take a look at who's driving the next time you see a semi or pickup with Naked Lady Mudflaps. I don't think you're going to see a woman behind the wheel. Unless, of course, she just borrowed the truck.

None of which has anything to do with my reason for choosing Naked Lady Mudflaps as the title of this chapter. I just liked the way the words sound.

Now, this is not about equality. In no way should it be taken to mean that I do not believe in equal pay for equal work, and equal rights under the law. I do. I think that men and women should absolutely be treated as equals, even though they are not, not by a long shot. In my experience, women are superior in almost every meaningful way.

Yes, a woman made me write that. No, it was not my mother.[2]

Anyway, "equal" does not mean "same."

Let's take the practice of sharing. Women, as a rule, love to share things, especially desserts. You watch the next time you're in a restaurant and twelve women are dining together. Come the end of the meal, they will find a way to split a piece of cheesecake twelve ways. That way, everyone gets to have some dessert.

Men do not share the sharing impulse. Put twelve men in the same restaurant and come the end of the meal, you are not going to see twelve men sharing dessert. You will see twelve desserts. That's the man way to solve the dessert problem. It's not that we don't want everyone to have dessert. We do. We want everyone to have his own individual dessert. And we also expect everyone to keep their forks away from ours.

Women also share clothes. I can guarantee you men do not do this. Why? Because, being men, we are more than aware of one another's hygienic deficiencies. This, in fact, may be the single most important thing a guy learns in junior high gym class. Certainly it serves him better throughout his life than learning how to leave an angry welt on the back of someone's leg with a hard-thrown volleyball. (Dodge ball: The Great Crippler Of Seventh Graders.)

Anyway, about the most I can imagine a guy borrowing from another guy

---

[2]It was my Aunt Sharon.

would be a necktie. Anything else would just be too intimate.

Which gets us to another difference between men and women: Intimacy. Not sex. Guys are all in favor of sex, which explains the proliferation of certain Web sites, not to mention all those gentlemen's clubs where the behavior is frequently anything but gentlemanly. I am talking about intimacy, which often is the price a man has to pay for sex. Either that, or he has to get his household chores done first.

The other price, of course, is when he goes to one of those aforementioned gentlemen's clubs, where the cover charge is outrageous, the Cokes are five dollars each, and every close encounter with a scantily dressed female is intended to vacuum the money out of his wallet. Not that I know about this personally, you understand. Some other guys told me about it.

So why do guys go to gentlemen's clubs? Well, for starters, the women are in a state of undress. Men like that (see above under "Mudflaps"). And the encounters are in fact a business transaction, which means they are close, but not intimate. Guys are generally against intimacy. It often leads to sharing.

Women share much more than desserts. They are also big on sharing experiences, which could explain why they seem to be incapable of going to the restroom by themselves.

There are lots of things men enjoy doing with other men, but going to the can is generally not one of them.[3] This probably goes back to junior high gym class as well. Whatever the reason, women and their come-one, come-all restroom habits are something that men find absolutely confounding. Which is probably why women do it.

So what goes on in there? You've got me. I have no way of knowing. I'm a man. I can tell you, however, what men *believe* goes on when all the women at a table get up to visit the restroom *en masse*. Men believe the women are:

A. Talking about them, as in discussing how handsome and debonair they are. Which is unlikely.

B. Talking about them, as in discussing what dorks they are. Which is likely.

---

[3]Unless they're outside after a night of heavy drinking, in which case the more the merrier.

C. Talking about them, as in how much better-looking the men at the next table are. Which is usually true.

D. Talking about them, as in they are trying to figure out how to get rid of them so they can skip out with the men from the next table. Which is particularly upsetting to men who are married.

E. *Not* talking about them. Which is even worse.

This brings us around to another difference between men and women. I believe men and women are insecure in roughly equal amounts, which is to say hugely. The difference is women deal with insecurity by just going ahead and letting the world know they are insecure. On *Oprah*, if they can manage it.

Meanwhile, men deal with insecurity by being ridiculous.

My pal Frank and I have talked about this. We've both spent a lot of time in bars and honky tonks, and as a consequence have seen a good many bar fights between men. And every single fight we can recall has been over a woman. That, my friends, is really insecurity writ large. Well, insecurity mixed with a great deal of alcohol.

Now, this is not to say that women don't do the same dumb things. We've seen women fight over men as well, but I'd put the ratio at about nine to one, men over women. By my count, then, we have a clear statistical lead where appalling behavior is concerned.

In recent years, I have become most aware of the differences between men and women where food is concerned. Every woman I know has food issues of one sort or another. I don't think I have ever heard that phrase—"food issues"—coming out of a man's mouth, unless of course he was complaining about a woman, as in, "My wife says we can't have cheese in the house because she'll eat it. She has food issues."

You see, to a man's mind, the reason you *have* cheese in the house is to eat it. And the only food issue is when there's not enough of it.

I know women who will sit down and eat something they absolutely hate, something that practically makes them gag, because it's supposed to be good for you. I have never seen a man do this, and I have seen men eat some pretty disgusting stuff. Men will, however, sit down and deliberately eat something that is bad for them, usually to make a point: Go ahead and choke down those

Brussels sprouts if you want to, dear. I'll just have a triple cheeseburger.

I learned a long time ago not to let a woman pick up lunch for me. A female co-worker at the newspaper once offered to bring me a sandwich, and I agreed. She asked what I wanted on it. I said ham and cheese. I then went back to work figuring that some time in the near future, I would be eating a ham and cheese sandwich.

Now, I am willing to admit that what happened next was partly my own fault for not being specific. I also believe, however, that it says something about the girl approach to food.

I had expected a guy sandwich, which is to say something made of rye bread, ham, cheese, and mustard. What I got instead were two rather thickish slices of some sort of seven-grain particle board. Between them was a smear of cream cheese, a piece of ham about the size and thickness of a playing card, and a big wad of sprouts. Sprouts I find particularly objectionable. Sprouts are not food. Sprouts are grass.

What I got was a girl sandwich.

I also do not let women order my pizza. I am a purist where pizza is concerned. I like mine rather plain. A simple cheese and tomato pizza is fine with me, and if I'm feeling decadent, I have them add pepperoni. I happen to think that where pizza is concerned, less is indeed more.

Women I have known, however, see pizza as something that needs to be accessorized, with artichoke hearts, and spinach, and goat cheese, and arugula, which is unique among vegetables in that it is the only one with a name that sounds like an old-fashioned car horn. I don't see the point in this kind of gussied-up pizza. If a salad is what you want, then that's what you should order. Don't make the pizza suffer because you have food issues.

The city where I make my home, I am happy to say, is mostly a guy town as far as restaurants are concerned. By that I mean there are an awful lot of places in Indianapolis where you can go for nice, thick pieces of beef, in large cuts that look like they came from an episode of *The Flintstones*. Indianapolis has, I believe, about one steak house for every five hundred male residents. This means that every man in Indianapolis could go out for a steak every night of his life if he wanted to. Not that he would want to. Man does not live by steak alone, you know. Sometimes he prefers fried chicken.[4]

OK, enough about food. Let us now turn our attention to what really separates men and women: Monster truck rallies.

No, wait. That's not it. Kids, leave the room. This next part is for grown-ups. It's S-E-X.

It has been said that men think of sex once every eleven seconds or so. I don't know if I believe that. It seems kind of low to me.

Now, that does not mean that a man wants to have sex every eleven seconds or so. My goodness, nothing could be further from the truth. It would be strange indeed if once every eleven seconds, men suddenly stopped whatever they were doing to have sex. We'd never finish our steaks, for one thing.

No, just because men think of sex every eleven seconds or so does not mean men are in pursuit of sex every eleven seconds or so. Statistics show that men are in pursuit of sex every waking second of every day.

Women, on the other hand, do not think of sex every eleven seconds or so. Women's brains are programmed to think about something other than the biological imperative. Such as food issues. Although, now that I think about it, those probably have something to do with sex in some way, so strike that. Women think of sex as often as men. They just disguise it as a craving for cheese.

Another area where I have found men and women to be completely different is in the workplace. Now, granted, I spent most of my work life in newspaper offices, so it's not like I spent any significant time in a *real* workplace, but I think it was close enough for the purposes of illustration.

Understand that a newspaper office is usually home to a bunch of outsized egos (there's that insecurity thing again) that spend a good part of each day careening around the room, crashing into each other, with the expected results: Conflict. The men, as a rule, seemed not to mind it. They accepted it as part of the working conditions. The women, on the other hand, were concerned with eliminating it. The women were probably right, but the men would never admit that, so the attempts to eliminate conflict usually just ended up creating more of it.

Where this really came into question was in the distribution of the one

---

[4]I just had a thought. You *do* realize I'm kidding, don't you?

fringe benefit there never seems to be enough of: Recognition. Men seemed more able to accept the fact that in a product like a newspaper, some people are going to get attention for what they do and some are not. A lot of women I worked with had a problem with this.

I think this is something genetic, a condition planted in our makeup back in the caveman days. If I were to take the work dynamic I knew and apply it to the Clan of the Three-Toed Sloth, it would come out something like this:

The men, all thirty-six of them, meet in the morning and decide to go hunting. This is what they do. They go out and kill something and bring it back for the tribe to eat. They head out of the village and before long find a mastodon. Ralph[5] throws a spear. It misses. Phil[6] throws a spear. It hits. The mastodon dies. The thirty-six men drag it back to the cave where Phil is hailed as a hero, Ralph is teased for his ineptitude, and the other thirty-four wait for tomorrow when perhaps they'll have a chance to be a hero. Of course, it doesn't work this way. Phil is far and away the best mastodon-killer in the tribe, and chances are he'll kill tomorrow's mastodon just like he killed today's. Everybody knows this, and accepts it, albeit grudgingly to some degree. The important thing, ultimately, is that someone will kill the thing—probably Phil—and the tribe will have food.

OK, let's shift gears:

The women meet, all thirty-six of them, and decide to go hunting. They go out and find a mastodon. So far, so good. But this is where things take a turn.

Does Maxine[7] throw a spear and miss? Doesn't matter. Does Eleanor[8] throw a spear and hit? Also doesn't matter. What *does* matter is that the women make sure that all thirty-six women get to throw a spear, in order to keep things fair and to make sure nobody gets a big head like Phil.

It's not a very good way to hunt mastodons. Well, I can't say for sure because I never hunted mastodon. I used to hunt squirrels when I was a kid but I don't think that applies. But I think we can all see that the result, should all the women possess throwing arms of average accuracy and strength, would be one perforated mastodon. Not to mention one extremely puzzled Phil.

---

[5]Not his real name.

[6]Or his.

[7]Real name.

[8]Likewise.

Now let's leave the workplace and enter the home. Once again, we find numerous ways to prove our point that men and women are different.

Closets, for example. In closets we find clothes, and in clothes we find a stunning example of how our brains just work differently. It's on the tags, where the sizes are printed.

Women's clothes are sized in a secret code, a meaningless—to a man, anyway—jumble of words and numbers that appear to be intended not to indicate what size the clothes are, but what size the wearer wishes the clothes to be.

For example, I recently read that the so-called American women's average size eight (an average which is disputed by nearly every woman I know) is in fact what used to be called a size ten. The size of the garment didn't change. The manufacturers just lowered the number.

Not only that, but the size varies from manufacturer to manufacturer. What is a size ten from one clothing maker is a size twelve at another.

Then, as if the numbers weren't confusing enough, you have the size names to contend with: Petite, Junior, Misses', Women's (aren't they all women?), Petite Miss, Junior Woman, Woman Petite, Junior Mint, Plus Size, Mutiplication Size, and Don't Ask.

The sizing of men's clothing is very straightforward. You measure a man's dimensions—neck, chest, sleeve, waist, inseam—and that's what size he takes. Or, if you're disinclined to do that much work, you can eyeball it and go with the generalized sizes—small, medium, large, extra large, extra-extra large, and King Kong. Doesn't matter, as long as it fits. We're not trying to fool anybody, which is why you will never, ever hear one man ask another "Does this outfit make my butt look big?"

The objective of sizing is to achieve some sort of general standard. In one instance, the sizing of women's clothing succeeds admirably. It is generally held as standard knowledge that men will not be able to figure it out, and that whenever we attempt to buy clothing for a woman, we will get it wrong. It will either be too large, too small, or, in the case of lingerie, too embarrassing. Men and women have way different ideas on what constitutes suitable lingerie. Basically, men like something made of three doilies and some ribbon. And not big doilies, either. To tell you the truth, we're lucky women don't have an equivalently embarrassing thing they can buy for men on Valentine's Day.

Whatever we get, nine times out of ten we will wind up feeling like dopes, which may have been the objective all along.

Let us adjourn now to the bathroom, which is to a woman as a garage is to a man: Full of highly specialized tools and materials that are mysterious to the opposite sex.

We're looking at a standard, two-sink bathroom. The sink on the right hand side has been designated his. Around it we find a toothbrush, toothpaste, razor, shaving cream, aftershave, a bar of soap, some deodorant, a comb, and a hand towel—pretty straightforward stuff.

The sink on the left is hers. Around it we find a toothbrush and toothpaste; several sponges of various textures and sizes; four little soaps in the shapes of sea creatures, which have never been used, in a bowl shaped like a scallop shell; three squeeze tubes of hair-care products; several pots, tubes, and bottles of cleansers, pastes, deodorants, moisturizers, exfoliants, weedkillers, and scents, most of which are derived from plant matter, peach pits, and other things which used to be considered rubbish; various instruments for tweezing, pluck-ing, curling, igniting, and sandblasting; cotton balls; three or four different types of paint remover; and seven mismatched earrings.

The bathtub is even worse. A guy might be lucky if he can find room for his one bottle of shampoo, what with all the cleansers and lotions and loofas and shampoos and conditioners and moisturizers and bath salts and bubble fluids.

And that's just for one night at the hotel.

As you might have surmised, I have been dealing with this business of men and women being different for a long, long time. I first became aware—I mean, really aware—of the difference between males and females in the sixth grade. Her name was Elizabeth Robinson.

Elizabeth could hit a baseball farther than most of the boys in class. She could whistle louder than all of us. She had what we then called "spunk" and we now call "attitude," which is to say Elizabeth didn't take any lip off anybody.

She also had wavy, flaming red hair[9] and her physique was already showing some interesting contours beneath the blue plaid of her Our Lady of Lourdes uniform.

Now, she was not the neighborhood va-va-voom girl. That was Wanda Akey, who had long, straight brown hair and contours on the same lines as Elizabeth

Robinson's, although on a frame about six inches shorter. Which, now that I think about it, made her a little on the pudgy side, although we didn't know it then. Wanda said she was built and we accepted it at face value.

Wanda batted her eyes at seventh- and eighth-grade boys when they walked past us in the lunch line. It was rumored that she had been known to "make out" and have birthday parties, to which no sixth grade boy was invited, in which bottles were spun and post office played. She had an older sister, also pudgy, who wore extremely short and tight miniskirts when she came by school with her boyfriend, who had a loud car, to take Wanda home. Wanda's ambition was to be a movie star, and in every class picture, she always had her head cocked to one side because, she said, that's what movie stars did.

We boys put it all together and decided on the face of this overwhelming evidence that Wanda was a sexpot.

Actually, I didn't think much of Elizabeth or Wanda either one at that point. I was coming out of kidhood, but I wasn't yet a teenager, and so I wasn't really equipped, mentally, emotionally, or hormonally, to take in that kind of information. At that point in my life, my number one interest was the guitar. Number two was comic books.

All that changed one day after school. I was walking home, minding my own business, when KA-POW! Someone smacked me in the back of the head.

I turned around and there was Elizabeth Robinson.

"Hiya, Red-MAN," she said, knowing how much I hated being called Red-MAN.

"It's not Red-MAN. It's Red-MOND," I said, bearing down hard on that second "d."

"Same difference," she said, shrugging. She was walking alongside me now.

"You hit me."

"Brilliant deduction, Sherlock." I *told* you she had spunk.

"Why did you hit me?"

"You looked like you needed it." And with that she peeled away and went down her street, leaving me four blocks to walk home along and wonder just what on earth had gotten into Elizabeth Robinson.

---

[9]Remember those mudflaps? The ones with the woman I always presume to be a redhead? I think I see a pattern developing.

The next day I found out. Helen Gregory, Elizabeth's best friend, sidled up to me in the lunchroom. "Elizabeth likes you," she said.

I decided, right then and there, that I liked Elizabeth Robinson too. It seemed kind of weird. I mean, weren't you supposed to spend months mooning over someone before you came out and declared your like? Weren't you supposed to carve initials in a tree, or at least print them with your cartridge pen on the blue fabric cover of your looseleaf binder? Weren't you supposed to see a shimmering aura around the face of your beloved everytime you looked at her? I was looking at Elizabeth and she was eating fish sticks. No aura.[10]

So Elizabeth and I became an item. Not that you could prove it by me. For me, life went on pretty much as it always had—I did the same things with my friends that I had done all along. Likewise for Elizabeth. The only difference between us as an item and us in our pre-item days was that she now felt free to run up behind me on the way home from school and whack me on the back of the head every afternoon. And I can remember thinking that this didn't seem like romance, at least as I understood it from movies and pop songs. None of them mentioned headaches.

Elizabeth and I had exactly one date. We went to a movie. It was a Saturday feature (two Dracula movies) at the Bethesda Theater in Bethesda, Maryland. She sat with her friends and I sat with mine. Now that I think about it, it wasn't so much a date as a coincidence.

The following Monday, Helen Gregory sidled up again and said Elizabeth didn't like me anymore. To tell the truth, I was kind of relieved, but at the same time puzzled—which, I must admit, has pretty much been the case for me, where women are concerned, ever since.

But it taught me a valuable lesson. It taught me that for all we have in common—and we do have a lot in common—men and women are very different creatures indeed, and maybe we're not supposed to understand how the other half works. Maybe we're just supposed to accept them, as they accept us, and celebrate the difference. Perhaps with a steak.

---

[10]Your results may vary.

———————|———————

TEN

The Night the Wheels Fell off Roy D. Bone

Once or twice a year, my friend Frank Dean's phone will ring in the middle of the night—three, four in the morning—and he always knows who is calling. It's Roy D. Bone, checking in from somewhere in the world. Florida. Canada (usually one of the western provinces). Kansas, or one of those other rectangular states.

"Frank Dean," Roy will say. "Frank Dean." He isn't saying it as a question, the way you might if you were calling someone and you weren't sure you recognized the voice—*Frank Dean? Hey, for a second there it didn't sound like you.* It's a statement, flat and declarative and final, with a pause between syllables for effect and a little extra weight put on that last one so as to drive it home: "Frank … Dean."

Now, I'm just hazarding a guess here, but if it were your phone ringing in the middle of the night, if you found yourself yanked out of a sound sleep just to hear someone tell you something you already know—that is, who you are—you probably wouldn't like it. I wouldn't. And Frank wouldn't either, if the person on the line were anyone other than Roy D. Bone.

Roy D. Bone is a genius, a certified, gold-plated, one-of-a-kind hillbilly genius. You can forgive a lot when you're dealing with one of those. Frank does. He always did, and I think he always will.

"There's only one Roy D. Bone," Frank says.

Then he adds: "I don't think the world could handle two."

I still remember the first time I heard about Roy D. Bone. I was a music critic at *The Indianapolis News* and, as such, had developed a tremendous way to get out of work when I didn't feel like sticking around the office. I would tell the boss I was doing research, and then go hang out at Frank's guitar shop on the East Side of Indianapolis.

Well, it was research of a sort. Frank and I and whoever else happened to wander into the store would sit around and play guitars and listen to records and talk about music. I was broadening my understanding of music, you see.

How could I intelligently comment on the qualities of the Fender Telecaster guitar, for example, unless I actually pulled one off of the display, plugged it in, and played along while Frank sang Johnny Cash songs? Really, I was doing it for the reader, when you think about it. At least, that's the excuse I had prepared in case anyone ever asked me just what the hell I was doing with my afternoons.

People who see us together think Frank and I have been friends all our lives, and we don't do much to discourage that belief. Frank tells people we're brothers by different sets of parents, and I don't think I've ever called his mother anything other than "Mom." But the truth of the matter is, Frank and I have only known each other about twenty years.

We knew of each other before we met. I was, as I mentioned, the music critic for *The News*, which gave me a certain amount of visibility. Frank was a musician—by acclamation the best country songwriter in town, maybe the best songwriter period. He still is, as far as I'm concerned. He was known for his saturnine disposition, a low tolerance for foolishness, and a withering wit that was equal parts *Hee-Haw* and Groucho Marx. It was really only a matter of time before we became friends.

Our introduction was arranged by our mutual acquaintance Rene Arbuckle, who had known and admired Frank for years. One day she took me to his store and more or less turned us loose on each other.

I was studying the display of used records for sale, the *O* section in particular, when Frank sidled up next to me and said, in his low, conspiratorial voice:

"You like Buck Owens?"

I was being tested.

"Of course," I said. "Buck Owens and the Buckaroos were a great rock and roll band that just happened to play country music."

It was the right answer. And it was something I deeply believed (and still do). I love Buck Owens and the Buckaroos almost as much as Frank does.

Frank and I became fast friends at that very moment, and it remains one of the proudest moments of my life.

The first music I can remember loving was country music. In fact, the first concert that really and truly impressed me was a Grand Ole Opry show at the Indiana state fairgrounds coliseum in the early 1960s (Dad got free tickets).

The headliners were Ernest Tubb and the Texas Troubadours, and they made an impression that lasts to this day. They were wearing turquoise and lavender cowboy suits and they played twangy, swingy music that wiped out the memory of any other concert I had seen up to that point. Well, come to think of it, there was only one, a performance by Fred Waring and his Pennsylvanians. Dad got free tickets for that, too. And no offense, Fred Waring fans, but Fred Waring music does nothing for me. I like his blenders, though.

I remained an Ernest Tubb fan right up until the moment I saw the Beatles on the Ed Sullivan Show. Then, being the fickle sort of ten-year-old I was, I forgot all about E.T. and aligned myself with the Beatles camp. A few years later, though, I began to listen again to country music. Bend an ear, kiddies, because this is where it gets good. Back then, you see, the good radio was on the AM cycle. Yes, I said the AM cycle, where all the loudmouths are today. Well, back then, FM was for the sort of music you only heard in dentists' offices. You tuned to AM for the good stuff.

And what made it really good was the fact that, unlike today, they didn't have any kind of rules about what music goes where. It was possible, in a half-hour of radio listening, to hear the Beatles, the Rolling Stones, George Jones, Tammy Wynette, Otis Redding, and Aretha Franklin. On the same station. It was broadcasting in the truest sense of the word.

Understand now, kids, that I am not talking about the too-slick, country-hunk-and-diva pop music that passes for country music today. I am talking about the real deal, the unvarnished twang thang, the classic drinkin' and cheatin' songs (or, as Frank calls them, "alcoholism and adultery you can dance to").

This is the sort of thing Frank and I used to discuss when I went to his store. Actually, it's still the sort of thing we discuss. That and politics. And religion. And old TV shows.

Anyway, it's what I was expecting one afternoon when I wandered in and found Frank still marveling at something he had seen the night before.

At the time, Frank was leading a classic-country band called Hillbilly Central, and they were regular winners of a battle of the bands going on somewhere down on the south side of Indianapolis. The night before, they had placed second. The winner was some guy nobody had ever seen before, a slick-haired, dark-eyed stranger who played piano, guitar, bass, and pedal steel, and whose big, strong, edge-of-heartbreak singing voice just about blew the windows out of their casements. The winner was Roy D. Bone.

Frank was already working on Roy to join Hillbilly Central.

"Wait till you hear this guy," he said. "He can stand there flatfooted and sing *He Stopped Loving Her Today* in the key of C and just light it up." For those of you who don't speak hillbilly musician, that means he's good.

My chance came to hear him a few days later, when Frank and the band turned up for their regular gig at the Who's Here, a little neighborhood tavern near downtown Indianapolis. It had a dedicated core of regulars for whom it was a true second home. As Frank likes to say, it was the kind of place where you could go set up your equipment at three and come back to play at nine to find the same people sitting on the same stools drinking the same drinks as they were six hours ago. That's why we liked it. It was real. No ferns.

As I recall, Roy was going to show up and sing a few in the band's second or third set. Before then, Frank gave me the rundown on the guy.

Roy, he said, came from central Ohio, where he was a kid gospel singer—made records, the whole bit. This is not suprising. Central Ohio is the Midwest Distribution Center for evangelists and gospel singers. It is also home to lots and lots of people who left the mountains of West Virginia looking for work and a better life.

Frank says they landed there because central Ohio is exactly one tank of gas from West Virginia. He ought to know. He's from West Virginia, too. I guess his family had enough for two tanks of gas, and that's how they came to Indianapolis.

Roy had only recently come to Indianapolis because his wife was in the Army, stationed at Ft. Benjamin Harrison, and had just that week started singing in public around the city.

Oh, and there was one other thing I needed to know, Frank said: "He's nuts."

Not bad nuts, you understand. Not the kind of nuts that hurts people. Roy was the kind of nuts you sometimes find in musicians, especially good musicians, especially good country musicians, the kind of nuts that acts on impulse almost 100 percent of the time. You know the old joke about the hillbilly's last words being "Hey, fellers, watch this!"? That kind of nuts.

The legend of Roy D. Bone has many examples of this behavior. My favorite concerns Roy's behavior the night that Ernest Tubb died. Roy was living in Nashville at the time, and when he heard the news he was heartbroken. I mean shattered. And so he made his way, weeping, to the Ernest Tubb Record Shop. I guess to Roy it just seemed like the thing to do.

You remember how record stores used to display albums in those big old cases that looked sort of like stretched-out doghouses? They had those there. Roy sat down at the end of one, out of the aisle and out of sight, and wept some more. He pulled his jacket over his head and cried himself to sleep.

A few hours later, he was awakened by the prodding toe of a cowboy boot. He pulled the jacket off his head and looked up, blinking. Standing over him were several members of the Texas Troubadors, who, like Roy, had found themselves pulled to the record shop when they learned of E.T.'s death. The store was closed and Roy, sleeping in a corner out of sight, had gone unnoticed when it came time to lock up.

The Troubadors helped him to his feet, and Roy joined the wake.

See? Nuts. But in a good way.

Roy was also the kind of nuts that lives in constant conflict because it loves Jesus and plays the devil's music (see any biography of Jerry Lee Lewis for more details on that one), and it only got worse when he drank. Which is why Roy tried not to drink, and for the most part succeeded.

He came in, sang a few songs, and, as Frank had predicted, blew everyone away with his talent. In fact, he may have been the single most talented local musician I ever saw. I'm not kidding. He was that good. His voice was strong, clear, and supple, with phenomenal range, from a warm Jim Reeves baritone to a piercing Bill Monroe tenor. He played superb honky-tonk piano. And, most impressive to me, he had mastered the pedal steel guitar, the most complicated and difficult instrument in country music.

To play the pedal steel requires the use of both hands, both feet, both knees, and an encyclopedic knowledge of chord structure. Invented by someone who obviously had too much time on his hands, plus a mild streak of sadism, it has (in its most common configuration) ten strings, three pedals, and two knee levers. The pedals and levels control the pitch of certain strings, creating new chords out of old ones and moving lines out of static ones. Quoting Frank once again, it is the guitar as reinvented by Rube Goldberg. Strong men, talented men, have been known to walk away weeping from simply trying to tune the damn thing.

Roy played it like a master. With his hands (and feet and knees) he made it sing with joy and cry with despair.

And on top of it all, he was a nice guy—friendly, a little bashful actually, unsure of his talents. That was the part that made us all wonder. Here was this guy who had more all-around musical talent than anyone we knew, and he didn't think he was all that good.

Roy soon joined the band, and he and I became … well, not friends in the sense that Frank and I were friends, but more than acquaintances. I was writing songs myself then, and I was working on one that I thought would be perfect for Roy. All I had was the hook—"Maybe the answer's at the bottom of the glass"—but Roy loved it. Every time he saw me he'd walk up, stick out a hand, and declare, "Mike … Redmond." And then he'd add, "Maybe the answer's at the bottom of the glass."

His favorite songwriter, though, was Frank. Roy was positively worshipful when it came to Frank's songs, especially "If I Were You," a classic country weeper that is loved by just about anyone who hears it, unless they run a record company. Then they say it's too country for today's country music.

Boy, did Roy love that song. He'd sing it five or six times a night if you'd let him. He thought Frank was the best songwriter since Stephen Foster. And that was what led to the on-stage meltdown known to those who saw it as The Night The Wheels Fell Off Roy D. Bone.

It was a Saturday night, and Roy had been with the band several months by then. When I walked into the Who's Here, he was standing at the bar with a small barrel of cognac in his hand. "Mike … Redmond," he declared. "Maybe the answer's at the bottom of the glass." He raised his snifter in salute, and then went looking for answers in one large gulp.

Why was he drinking? Who knows? Wife trouble, maybe. Work trouble (although, come to think of it, I never did hear Roy say anything about having a job). Or maybe it was just that old devil Impulse come around to stick Roy with his pitchfork that night. Whatever it was, it wasn't good. With some people, alcohol is an amplifier—it takes whatever they are and makes it louder. With Roy, it was an entire public address system.

The Who's Here had a full house that night—its usual core of daily regulars, plus the weekend familiars such as myself, and a bunch of newbies besides.

Word had begun to spread about Hillbilly Central, and it was attracting larger crowds each weekend—including some who came expecting to hear what they *believed* was country music, the cowboy-hat-and-starched-jeans music they heard on the radio, and were a little confused by the real thing as played by Hillbilly Central.

The first set went without incident. The band played, people danced, the cash register rang, and all was right with the world. During the break, Roy had two more cognacs.

About two songs into the second set, a table of newbies yelled to the stage that they wanted to hear something by Garth Brooks. Frank, surprisingly, ignored them. Remember what I said about low tolerance for foolishness? Asking a certified classic honky tonk band to play "Friends in Low Places" was the very *definition* of foolishness in the Frank dictionary. I have been there when people have made that kind of request, and I have watched as Frank, with a few laser-guided cracks, reduced them to quivering heaps. I have seen them go running to the restroom in tears, their friends trailing after them, faces etched with concern, the last one calling to the bandstand, "I have never seen anyone so mean in all my life!" And those were the guys.

But Frank was in a good mood and didn't say anything. The Garth fans must have taken this to mean he didn't hear them. Who knows, maybe he didn't. But Roy did.

"What did you say?" he called from the stage, his dark eyes scanning the crowd. "Garth Brooks? GARTH BROOKS? DID SOMEONE SAY THEY WANTED TO HEAR GARTH BROOKS?"

The other guys in the band just stood there, watching. They were as fascinated as the rest of us by Roy's sudden explosion.

"WE AIN'T GONNA PLAY NO GARTH (BAD WORD) BROOKS," Roy thundered. "GARTH BROOKS IS AN (SEVERAL BAD WORDS) WHO (A COUPLE OF REALLY BAD WORDS) AND ANYONE WHO WANTS TO HEAR GARTH BROOKS CAN (REALLY, REALLY, *REALLY* BAD WORD)."

He stalked around the stage for a few seconds, red-faced and furious. Steam was pouring from his ears. I swear to God. Hot clouds of vapor, shooting from each side of his head. Then he was back at the microphone:

"I SWEAR TO GOD!" he yelled. "I CAN'T BELIEVE YOU PEOPLE. RIGHT

HERE YOU GOT A SONGWRITER LIKE FRANK … DEAN, ONE OF THE BEST SONGWRITERS EVER, RIGHT HERE … AND YOU WANT TO HEAR GARTH (BAD WORD AGAIN) BROOKS."

He took a breath.

"Well, I ain't gonna stand for it. I just ain't. I AIN'T."

And with that, he packed up his steel guitar, slammed his keyboard into a case, picked them up, and stormed out the door.

A stunned silence settled over the Who's Here. Everyone—band, customers, servers, bartender—stood there, slack-jawed and goggle-eyed, at what we had just seen. And then Frank showed himself to be the professional that he truly is. A veteran of thousands of honky-tonks, he had seen this kind of behavior before. Heck, he might have even done it himself in his more hotheaded days. Frank shrugged, turned to the band, and counted off a song: "Goodbye's All We Got Left to Say," if memory serves.

What happened next is the object of some dispute among the witnesses. When we get together to talk it over these days, like veterans reliving a battle, it breaks down into two camps: Those who believe Roy stole a car, and those who need more evidence. I fall into the latter category. I mean, yes, a couple of regulars who left soon after Roy *did* come rushing back in to say their car was gone, but it was not at all unusual for patrons of the Who's Here to lose their cars. And then they would find them in the parking lot the next morning after they'd had some coffee and aspirin.

Whatever it was, Roy was gone. For a while, anyway. He came back to the bar as the band was finishing its last set—no less sober, but considerably less angry.

After apologizing to Frank, about twenty minutes' worth, he seated himself at a table, ordered another cognac, and sighed deeply.

Frank and I sat down at the table, Frank to Roy's right, me to his left. Ralph Jeffers, a fine honky tonk musician in his own right and possessed of a talent for put-downs himself, plopped himself into the chair opposite Roy.

"Boys, I'm a sinner," Roy said, tears in his eyes.

"Yes, you are," agreed Ralph.

"I mean, what am I doing in a place like this singing this kind of music?" asked Roy. "This ain't right. This ain't a godly life. This is a life of drinkin' and cheatin' and painted women and bad men, except for you fellers. I ain't supposed to be livin' this kind of life. I'm supposed to try to be like Jesus."

"You got me, Roy," said Ralph. "What *are* you doing in a place like this singing this kind of music?" Always a kind word, that Ralph.

"I'm sinnin', that's what I'm doing. Sinnin'. I'm a sinner, a worthless sinner. I'm sick with sin. If you was to crack me open I'd be full of sin like I was full of cancer."

"You covered that already," said the ever-helpful Ralph.

Frank and I didn't say a word. We were like spectators at a tennis match, swiveling our heads this way to see what Roy would serve, that way to see how Ralph would volley.

"I'm serious, boys. If Jesus came back tonight, I'd go to hell. Straight to hell. There ain't no room in paradise for a sinner like Roy D. Bone. He'd stand there at the gates of heaven and say, 'Get out of here, Roy D. Bone.' We ain't got no place for the likes of you. You said you took Jesus into your heart but you ain't nothin' but a lyin' sinner who drinks and plays the devil's music. Get on down to hell, Roy D. Bone, they're waitin' on you."

That's when we knew Roy was irretrievably gone, when he started referring to himself in the third person. It is a classic sign of someone who has started to lose his grip on his trombone slide, if you get my drift. Again, I refer you to Jerry Lee Lewis.

Ralph jumped in with more words of comfort: "You're right, Roy. You're going to hell. You will not pass Go, you will not collect two hundred dollars. You are going to fry for all enternity. Boy, do I feel sorry for you."

Back and forth they went like that for something like a half an hour, Roy getting drunker and more desperate, Ralph goading him on. It was the Wimbledon of bar discussions. Roy would send a Bible verse, or a snippet of a gospel song, over the net; Ralph sent it zinging back into Roy's court with a "Good God, man! Why don't you just end it now and put us all out of your misery?"

At about three in the morning, Frank and I gave up. A person can only take so much entertainment, after all. Besides, we knew that we had been witness to something special: An honest-to-goodness, heaven-or-hell, alcohol-fueled hillbilly meltdown. We had been there the night the wheels fell off of Roy D. Bone.

The night was not over for Ralph. They had to leave the bar and Roy didn't want to, or couldn't, go home, so Ralph took him back to his place to sleep it off. Except Roy didn't. He stayed there until dawn, smoking Ralph's cigarettes, drinking Ralph's booze, and playing every single one of Ralph's Hank Williams records while he paced around the living room, alternately cursing at himself and then apologizing to Jesus.

When Ralph woke up, he was gone.

I never saw Roy D. Bone again. He left town shortly thereafter. We heard that he was singing in a gospel group down south somewhere. Then we heard he was playing piano in a country band up north somewhere. And, like I said, once a year he'd make that middle of the night telephone call to Frank … Dean, just to say hello.

But he left his mark on us, that's for sure. We've never stopped talking about him, and we never will. He set a standard the rest of us can never exceed.

We may sing country music, or write country music, or listen to country music, but Roy D. Bone *was* country music.

ELEVEN

Drums Along the Malecon

I go to Cuba at least twice a year—in my dreams. Usually after I've eaten shrimp. I always dream vividly after I've eaten shrimp. And I do mean vividly—the colors, the details, the plots, the characters, everything is so bright and sharp and detailed that I wake up thinking it really happened, and being mildly disappointed it did not. And shrimp dreams stay with me, too. Usually I forget my dreams within minutes of awakening, but not shrimp dreams. Shrimp dreams linger in my memory banks for months and even years. I remember one in which a rather statuesque brunette … heh-heh. Excuse me. Let's just say that ever since I had this dream I have never missed an all-you-can-eat crustacean special at Red Lobster.

Oh well. What I do know is that shrimp somehow unlocks the door to my subconscious mind. And my subconscious mind spends quite a bit of time in Cuba.

I went to Cuba in 1994. Why? I could waste a whole bunch of ink and paper giving you a lot of high-flown prose about politics and journalism and the search for truth, but I'm not that good of a liar. I went to Cuba for three reasons:

1. A woman I had the hots for wanted to go there. The less said about that the better. And no, she wasn't brunette.
2. I like Cuban music. Once a Desi Arnaz fan, always a Desi Arnaz fan.
3. I wasn't supposed to.

Of the three, the last reason makes the most sense to me now. While I am not generally known as a risk-taker—I consult maps, check the tire pressure, cross with the green light, and keep a fire extinguisher handy, and that's just to go to the drugstore—I do resent being told I am not allowed to do something for reasons that I find ridiculous. Which is the word I use for U.S. foreign policy toward Cuba.

Without getting too political, it seems to me that forty-plus years should be God's plenty time to figure out that the embargo doesn't work—if, in fact, the intent of the embargo is to force Fidel Castro from power. For forty years we've been pushing, and you'll notice he hasn't budged.

If, on the other hand, the purpose of the embargo is to keep Fidel in power so he may always have a bogeyman to blame for Cuba's problem, thereby giving the U.S. a bogeyman at whom candidates can snarl in an attempt to win Cuban-American votes in Florida—well, in that case, it succeeds remarkably. Especially when Ralph Nader is running as a third-party presidential candidate.

Up to the point where it denies people in Cuba access to medicines, prohibits a free exchange of ideas and cultures, and robs American farmers of a valuable market, the isolation of Cuba is a joke. I once spent an evening in a Havana cocktail lounge listening to country music, smoking Marlboros, and drinking a Coke. Then I went back to my hotel room and watched CNN and read that day's *USA Today*. Hello? Someone said something about an embargo?

But that's politics, and as I said, not really what this is about. This is about how I came to find myself in a forbidden place—and how after seeing it once, I have never really left it.

I first thought to go to Cuba through official channels, as a journalist. For some reason, I thought the Cuban government would welcome a visit from a reporter from a dying afternoon newspaper in Indiana. I tell you this just to show you how stupid I can be sometimes.

The Cuban government, for some reason, had absolutely zero interest in getting stories and photos in *The Indianapolis News*. Imagine that. The people at the Cuban Interests Section (sort of an embassy-equivalent in Washington, D.C.) denied my request for a visa, although they were exceedingly polite about it, so much so that I wrote back to beseech them one more time. The second time, they didn't answer.

I decided, then, to go as a tourist and write about it when I returned. I did this with trepidation; in calling around to other reporters who had recently been to Cuba, they all told me the Cuban government took a dim view of this sort of end run around its visa restrictions. Great. Now whether I wanted it or not, I was an international man of intrigue. Well, it felt that way. Sort of.

It fell to me to make the travel arrangements. I did this by faxing a travel agent in the Bahamas to ask about excursions to Cuba. The agent faxed back a price list for hotel packages and these instructions: "See Milton or Lily at the Cubana de Avacion counter at the Nassau airport. Bring cash."

See Milton or Lily? That's it? I'm looking for a way to sneak into a place my government says is off limits, and to do this I simply walk up to an airline counter and ask for Milton or Lily? I was expecting hoops to be jumped through, papers to be filled out, affidavits to be sworn, fingerprints to be taken, *something* other than "go see this guy I know."

A few weeks later, I found myself in the Nassau airport. I made my way to the Cubana counter. "Can I help you?" asked the man in charge—"Milton," according to his nametag. Lily was standing next to him.

I made the arrangements—four days in the Nacional hotel in Havana, three days at a Melia hotel in the resort town of Varadero. The price came to something like eight hundred dollars per person. I produced a wad of hundred-dollar bills and counted them out to Milton. He wrapped them around a bankroll the size of a small cabbage, which he then tucked into his shirt pocket, gas-station-attendant style.

I took a seat in the lounge to await the charter flight to Cuba, scheduled to leave at four P.M., which, I later learned, is the way Cubans say "7:45."

I passed the time in the airport scoping out my fellow travelers. A couple of big, beefy, Midwestern businessman types; a few suave South Americans; and, over in a corner, a gaggle of boisterous German college students on holiday, clad in the official uniform of German college students on holiday: tank tops, shorts, sandals, backpacks, and a stunning case of collective body odor. They all seem to be named Willie and Franz and when they weren't shouting to each other about how much fun they were going to have at the beach, they were shouting into cell phones about how much fun they were going to have at the beach.

At their periphery was a dark-haired guy dressed the same as the others, but instead of shouting he seemed to be talking on his cell phone, quietly and constantly. "I'll be damned," I thought. "A quiet German."

Remember this guy. We'll come back to him, or rather, he'll come back to us.

The plane arrived, a stunning example of late 1950s Soviet aviation technology, coughing blue smoke from its engines as the propellers shuddered to a stop. Suddenly I did not have a lot of confidence in the ability of this plane to get all the way from Nassau to Havana. Check that. I did not have a lot of confidence in the ability of this plane to get to the end of the runway.

It did not get better when we boarded. Stepping into the airplane, I cracked my skull on the bulkhead, hard, and I do mean hard. I took my seat with little cartoon stars and birdies doing orbits around my head and a fog settling over me. The stars and birds went but I became a little concerned when the fog did not.

Then it dawned on me that this was Soviet air conditioning—a fine spray of mist with a temperature only slightly lower than the ambient temperature of the airplane, which I would estimate to be about 120 degrees Fahrenheit. Basically, we were sitting in a rainstorm inside the airplane. Either that, or they were spraying the inside of the plane for bugs, which wouldn't have been a bad idea. I shared my seat with two cockroaches on their way to spend some time with family in Santiago.

The pilots started the plane. I glanced to my right just in time to see a giant ball of flame shooting out of that side's engine. Again, not a confidence-booster.

The plane sped down the runway and grabbed air, and I was on my way to Cuba, wondering what the hell I had gotten myself into.

We landed in Havana and I took a tourist bus—differentiated from the Cuban people's buses by being clean, new, and most important, running—to the Nacional Hotel. It's a beautiful place, opened in 1930, the hotel where movie stars and presidents used to stay when they went to Cuba. I recommend you stay there, too. Walking into the lobby, all cool marble and amber light, is like stepping into an old movie. You half expect to see Humphrey Bogart in a linen suit sipping a Cuba libre in the cocktail lounge.

The next day, while walking around the neighborhood, my traveling companion (remember the non-brunette?) went one direction while I went another—we'd had a bit of a tiff, you see, which actually turned out to be a valuable lesson for me. If you want to know if you and someone are suited for one another, travel to another country together. You'll probably find out in pretty short order whether or not you can get along. As it turned out, we couldn't.

She came back from her excursion with something of great value, however, for which I am grateful still. She came back with Angel Luis Argudin, who would become an unforgettable friend.

She had met him while aiming a camera at an ice cream stand. "Take my picture!" he cried. "I'm so pretty!" And so she did.

Angel came back with her to the hotel. Don't read anything into this. He was not a jinetero, the Cuban name (it means "jockey") for street hustler. He was merely following a custom I ran into frequently in Cuba: Ask a Cuban for directions, and chances are he'll just take you to wherever it is you're going, whether it's down the block or across the city. It's a charming custom. It's also sensible when dealing with gringos who don't know east from west and whose Spanish stops at the "Donde esta la biblioteca?" level.

Angel introduced himself to me. "Mucho gusto," I replied.

"Ah, you speak Spanish!" he said.

"Donde esta la biblioteca?" I answered.

We asked Angel if he would show us around Havana. He said he would be delighted. And so for the next three days, he guided us through his city, introduced us to his friends, taught us how to spot plainclothes cops (shiny shoes), interpreted for us, and kept the hustlers at bay.

We tried to pay Angel for his time. He would have nothing of it. All he wanted was to eat ice cream in the cafeteria of the Nacional Hotel. Which turned out to be damn near impossible. The hotel was for tourists and their dollars, and that made it off-limits to most Cubans.

We learned this the hard way when we tried to take Angel in with us. A cop stopped him at the hotel entrance, and before long, he and Angel were engaged in a furious debate.

Have you ever seen two angry Cubans debating? You non-Cubans, I mean. It's memorable. Their arms wave like untended fire hoses, and their Spanish—which, being Cuban Spanish, is rapid to begin with—kicks into overdrive. I tried to get in on it myself, but when two Cubans are going at it the way Angel and this cop were going at it, there's not much room for "Donde esta la biblioteca?"

My traveling companion (remember the blonde?) told me to keep my big American nose out of it and went into the hotel. Two minutes later she was back with a manager who told the tourist cop to let Angel pass. Later, I asked her what she had done.

"I just told him that either he could let Angel in, or we would be checking into another hotel and taking our money with us," she said. Capitalism triumphed that day.

Once inside, we told Angel to get anything he wanted from the menu. We were sure he would be hungry—this was the Special Period, as they called it in Cuba, when the economy was bottomed out thanks to the dissolution of the Soviet Union. All over Havana, people complained about food shortages. But all Angel wanted was ice cream.

"Ice cream is my life," he said. "I love you, ice cream." And he kissed the spoon.

The next day was another tiff day (see what I mean about traveling with someone?) and so Angel and I set off on our own in a taxi. I had in mind to see a few neighborhoods, maybe take some pictures of kids playing baseball, that sort of thing. At the mention of baseball, the cab driver perked up.

He said something to Angel, seated in the front passenger seat. Angel turned to me and said, "He wants to know your favorite baseball team."

Playing the odds, I lied and said the New York Yankees. I figured if any team had a following in Cuba it was probably the Yankees, seeing as how the Washington Senators (my kidhood favorites, who incidentally had a lot of Cuban players on the roster) were no more.

The cab driver lit up. "Bay Rute!" he said. Babe Ruth.

"Mickey Mantle," I answered.

"Lou Gerrih!" Gehrig.

"Joe Dimaggio!"

"Ay, si! Dimayo!"

Which was right about the time it started to rain, and I mean a real tropical storm, the kind that floods streets and fills the gutters *instantly*, where the rain comes down not in sheets but in roaring waves. The driver stopped in the middle of the street, rain hammering down all around us, and turned again to Angel with another question.

"He wants to know if you know anything about Cuban baseball," Angel said.

"Good pitching, good gloves and arms up the middle, lots of speed," I said. More Spanish.

"Do you know Omar Linares?" Angel asked.

I told him the truth: I knew a little about Omar Linares—third baseman, hellacious hitter, the best player in Cuba at the time—but not much more.

More Spanish.

"He said Omar Linares is the best hitter he has ever seen with a unique way to hold the bat," Angel reported.

Evidently I did not show sufficient comprehension, because the driver opened his door, jumped out into the rain, opened *my* door, gestured for me to step out with him, and proceeded to demonstrate for me the peculiarities of the Linares batting stance, with the bat cocked in such a way that the barrel is almost pointing back at the pitcher.

It remains one of my favorite memories: A cab driver who didn't speak English, a passenger who barely spoke Spanish, having a lively pantomimed conversation about baseball in a downpour.

I tried to return the favor by demonstrating the batting stance favored by Frank Howard, my favorite Washington Senator of the 1960s: hands held low, down by the right hip, the barrel of the bat pointing straight up. The driver was polite, nodding as if he were interested, but I think it lost something in the translation.

Angel, you notice, did not get out of the car. I asked him why.

"I like football," he said.

When you come back from Cuba, the first thing your friends want to know is if you saw Fidel.

No.

They also want to know if anyone tried to indoctrinate you.

Also no.

Then they want to know if you brought back any cigars.

No comment.

The point, though, is that once you cover Fidel, Communism, and cigars, you've just about exhausted the curiosity of a lot of Americans where Cuba is concerned. I guess that's not surprising, but it still strikes me as ... well, ignorant.

Cubans know a lot more about us than we know about them. What's more, they like us. I can't count how many times I saw a look of surprise spread over someone's face when I told them I was from the U.S., and how they then told me, without fail, that while they didn't much care for our government, they loved the American people.

Angel peppered us with questions about the U.S. He was needlessly insecure about his English and wanted to bolster it with the latest American slang. Unfortunately, he was asking the wrong guy on that one. However, if someday you find yourself in Cuba and a native comes up to you and says something is groovy, you'll know I was not without influence down there.

Angel wanted to know about films and books. He wanted to know about food. He was staggered to learn that there are sometimes two or even three ice cream shops in the same mall. Come to think of it, he was also staggered by the idea of a mall.

He wanted to know why American politicians hated Cuba, why we just couldn't admit our differences and try to get along. I didn't even try to answer that one.

He expressed admiration for Fidel—not uncommon or surprising, especially among Cuba's blacks, such as Angel. More than any other group, theirs was the standard of living that increased the most after the revolution. Sons and daughters of peasants became doctors and scientists in one generation. In fact, there's a saying in Cuba along the lines of, "If you can find a black doctor who was educated before the revolution, hang on to him, because only a genius could get into medical school then, if he was black." He did *not*, however, express the same admiration for the Cuban government.

Take the Special Period, for example, when Cubans were called upon to make sacrifices of foods and comforts in order to get the economy jump-started. "It's just a plan," he said. "They do this all the time. We follow it for five years. Maybe it works. Probably it doesn't. So they make another plan."

As he talked, he engaged in a sign language particular to Cuba. For instance, as often as not he would not say the name "Fidel," but indicate it by stroking his fingers downward from his chin, as if stroking a beard. And instead of saying "government," "authorities," or "cops," he would tap two fingers on his shoulder, as if to indicate epaulets. And often, he would wink. Cubans are about the winkingest people I ever saw. They use it to indicate jokes, to indicate friendship, to indicate confidentiality. Either that, or there was an epidemic of nervous tics when I was there.

Angel was worshipful of Che Guevara, the revolution's secular saint, the pro-totypical new man, if you believe the hype (which is everywhere; where we have billboards, Cuba has slogans, and Che's visage stares down from any number of them). "Che was the greatest man," he said simply. "I love you, Che."

Angel did *not* want to hear about American music. A singer in a quartet at a hotel, he was convinced of the superiority of Cuban music to anything else on the planet, which, of course, is absolutely correct. And not only is it superior, it's everywhere. Every hotel, every bar, every restaurant, every street corner in Havana had a combo playing. In fact, some of the best music I heard popped up out of nowhere when two groups of musicians, walking toward each other on the Malecon, Havana's grand seaside promenade, stopped and began to jam. I'm not kidding you, it was all good—son, rumba, cha-cha-chá. I can hear it even now.

Most of the time, Angel and I rode around in private cars instead of cabs, and great cars they were, too. Old Chevys and Fords and Chryslers from the 1950s, kept running by the most ingenious mechanics in the world. There being a lack of spare parts, they frequently have to fashion their own, or fit parts from another make and model entirely onto an antique Detroit engine. I saw one old Pontiac that had to be at least 90 percent parts from a Lada, a crappy, un-derpowered Russian car. Somehow, it worked. It didn't go fast, but it ran.

Now, while I was doing all this wandering around looking at the sights, marveling at the old buildings and despairing at their disrepair, enjoying the hospitality of the people and despairing at their privations, I was trying to be a Double Secret Undercover Journalist as well. As far as anyone who saw me was concerned, I was just a sunburned North American with a nice camera. But be-neath the façade I was trying to memorize everything I saw. Then I would come back to my room at night and record everything in notebooks I kept stashed in my suitcase. I was still mindful of those "don't try the end run" warnings from the other reporters.

For this reason, I probably didn't enjoy Havana as much as I could have. I basked in its warmth but at the same time felt the chill of state security, real or imagined, watching me. Paranoia? Maybe. Maybe not, as you'll see.

You'll notice I haven't said much about Varadero. There's a reason for that. Varadero is a resort area, a spit of sugar-white sand upon which the Cuban government and its capitalist partners from other countries have built tourist hotels. It's like the Cuban version of Cancun. You go to Varadero when you want to go somewhere where you can be in Cuba without actually having any contact with Cubans.

No, it was Havana that stole my heart. Varadero just cleaned out my wallet. The only Cubans I saw there, besides hotel workers, were the young hookers—jineteras, girl jockeys, to use the vernacular—who had attached themselves to overweight, middle-aged European men for dollars and a chance to shop in the hotel's stores and eat in its restaurants. Sad.

I do recall one touching scene there, however. I had asked a hotel clerk for directions to the nearest Catholic church and a schedule of Masses, if he had it. He did, which surprised me—not because it was religion but because he actually had what I wanted when I wanted it. That hardly ever happens in Cuba.

At any rate, as he slid the paper across the counter to me he said, in a low voice: "Pray for us."

And then he winked.

Varadero also figured in what has become, over time, the most interesting and exciting part of trip, although I didn't think so back then.

The day before we (remember the blonde?) were scheduled to leave, the Cuban tourist ministry sent an official to the hotel, ostensibly to interview us on our trip and ask for suggestions for improvement. Really, her purpose was to make sure we were leaving as planned. I figured this out when she reminded us—three times—that the bus to take us to the airport would be at the hotel at 11:30 A.M. the next day.

At 11:30 on the dot, the bus pulled up. It was the first time I had seen anything in Cuba happen at the promised hour.

As I boarded, I noticed there was but one other passenger. Remember the guy with the cell phone at the Nassau airport? The one I thought was the only quiet German? It was him.

As I stashed my bag and took a seat, he smiled at me.

"Hello, Michael," he said. "Did you have a pleasant stay?"

Well.

My stomach flipped. I had never spoken to this man. I had seen him in the airport in Nassau and that was it. How did he know my name?

He introduced himself as Miguel and said he was from Miami. "I'm a private pilot," he added. "I fly down here all the time to get lobsters and stuff. I take them back to Miami and sell them."

Now, I was born in the morning, but it wasn't *that* morning. A private pilot just flying lah-de-dah into Cuban airspace any time he wanted? It didn't ring true to me.

Neither did it ring true to the other reporters I called when I returned home.

"He was your spook," one told me. "His job was to make sure you left the country when you were supposed to. He probably knew where you were the entire time."

When I dream of Cuba, I do not dream of Miguel the spook. I dream of Angel. I see him singing with a combo at the hotel, or singing along with those drummers and guitarists on the Malecon. I see him leading me through the throngs in Old Havana. And I see him again as I saw him last—standing in front of the hotel, screaming at me because I shoved a hundred dollars into his pocket.

"What is this?" he yelled. "What is this? Friends do not give money to friends. Friends give only friendship and it is enough."

He did keep the money, though.

I want to go back, soon. I want to see the place yet again before the inevitable happens. Yes, I do believe normalized relations between the U.S. and Cuba are inevitable, and I do believe they will come about sooner rather than later. And after that happens, the place will never be the same. I want to go back to Cuba before McDonald's gets there.

As it is, I can go back as a journalist. You see, as soon as I got back in 1994, I wrote a series of articles about the experience for *The News*. I think somebody at the Cuban Interests section must have read them and thought they were all right, because six weeks later, I got my visa. I still have it. Maybe I'll use it one of these days. In the meantime, I'll keep eating shrimp.

TWELVE

A Chicken Named Noodles

Really, all I wanted was chicken that tasted like chicken. I was tired of buying birds at the supermarket that were as flavorless as the Styrofoam they were packed in—unless, of course, they were half-rotten, in which case the Styrofoam was preferable. And probably better for you.

I just wanted to bite into a piece of fried chicken and have it taste the way it tasted when I was in a kid. Which, in case you missed it, was like chicken. You know, sort of like rabbit. And frog's legs. And squirrel, now that I think about it. Whatever it was, it was a far cry from what we get today. Of all the things that are said to taste like chicken, a modern supermarket chicken is pretty far down the list.

Anyway, I gave it some thought and hit upon what I thought was a perfect solution: Raising a few chickens up at the home place in LaGrange County. It's a farm, after all. Well, maybe a farmette, or *ferme petit*, or dinky little place miles from town would be a better description, seeing as the barn fell down and Mom sold off most of the acreage to our neighbor Jack, who planted Christmas trees on it. But still it's a place in the country with enough open area to raise something, and I thought that something ought to be chickens.

"Wouldn't it be great to have our own chickens?" I asked Mom.

"No," said Mom.

"But think," I said, "we could have chicken that actually tastes like"—here it comes again—"chicken."

"I don't care for chicken," said Mom.

"But what about chickens in the yard? Chickens in the yard make a place look homey. Don't you think it would be nice to have a few chickens running around the yard?"

"Oh, good Lord, no," said Mom. "When I was four years old the rooster flapped me. I haven't wanted to be around chickens ever since."

"I could come up on the weekends to take care of them," I added.

"Ha," said Mom.

OK, so you can see Mom was not exactly as excited about the idea as I had hoped.

Mom knew better than anyone what was going to happen, which is to say she was going to get stuck taking care of the chickens. She had history on her side, seeing as how she got stuck taking care of the dogs and cats and rabbits and goats and geese and any other nonhuman life form we kids brought home with us when we were little. Well, come to think of it, some human life forms as well. A few years ago my brother P.D. brought his pal Moose up for a visit, and Mom more or less adopted Moose. Which is good, because with another brother around, it means there's even less work for me to do when I visit. Also because Moose, whose actual name is Mark, is a really good guy.

Anyway, every time we solemnly promised to feed and water and tend to the animals, and every time it fell to Mom to make sure the animals were fed and watered and tended after we kids lost interest—usually at around the two-week mark. So when you think about it, it's her fault. She never should have let us keep any life form higher on the evolutionary ladder than sea monkeys.

Well, I wasn't done with the bird idea. I had an ace up my sleeve.

"You know what else would be good to have, Mom? Guineas."

She perked up. Mom has a weak spot for guineas. Well, that's not exactly right. Mom has a mortal fear of ticks and a seething hatred for Japanese beetles, and the prospect of a tick- and beetle-free yard hit Mom right where she lived. Ticks and Japanese beetles, you see, are like jelly beans and popcorn to guineas.

Guineas are also good watchdogs. Watchbirds. Feathered car alarms. Guineas will raise a ruckus whenever they're surprised, which is … well, constantly. The appearance of a strange figure in their proximity will set off a round of high-decible guinea shrieks. So will dogs, cats, horses, cars, trucks, tractors, airplanes, a shift in the wind, a one-degree change in the temperature, the rising of the sun, or the presence of another guinea. I said they were good watchbirds. I didn't say they were *smart* watchbirds.

It just occurred to me that some of you may not know what I'm talking about. Which wouldn't be the first time. Anyway, this would probably be a good time for us to have a little agriculture class. Today's lesson: What the Hell Is a Guinea?

Guinea fowl (*Numida meleagris*) originated in Africa untold eons ago, although they stopped evolving at a point where they were about half-lizard and half-bird, a sort of feathered iguana if you will, with a small vulture-ish head grafted onto a feathered football of a body. You Warner Brothers cartoon fans: I want you to think back to the cartoon when Bugs Bunny winds up on Mars, and Marvin Martian is going after him with two big Martian birds. Those birds, I am pretty sure, were modeled after guineas. (And people say you can't learn anything watching Saturday morning cartoons.)

Guineas used to be found on just about every Midwestern farm. My Grandma McKenzie had a flock of guineas around the place when I was a kid. We cousins remember them … well, I was going to say fondly, but that's not entirely accurate. My cousin Nate, for example, was reminiscing about them not too long ago.

"Those were the meanest damn birds," he said. Which is true. Grandma's guineas were mean. More than one kid ran screaming into the house when Grandma's guineas were on the loose and terrorizing anything that came into the yard, flapping and pecking and yelling. I don't know why they had all that attitude. Maybe they all had chips on their shoulders from being born guineas. If you were that ugly, you'd probably have an attitude, too. Or maybe Nate said something insulting to them. I wouldn't put it past him. At any rate, Grandma got rid of the guineas around 1960 or so and, speaking for the grandkids, we were all relieved.

You used to see guinea fowl on restaurant menus. It's quite good, richer than chicken without being gamy. Somewhere around here I have a book that includes a menu from the Rose Room of the Algonquin Hotel from 1929, at the time of the fabled Round Table. You could get a half a broiled guinea hen for $1.65. And remember the restaurant scene from the movie *The Bishop's Wife*, where Cary Grant (as the angel, Dudley) orders in French? Guinea hen.

Guinea hen still appears on plates, if not on menus. I was recently talking to a guy who raised guineas on a farm in Southern Illinois. He sold his birds to a restaurant supplier in Chicago. "And somewhere on the road from my house to Chicago," he said, "they magically turned into pheasants."

So, anyway, Mom was intrigued by the guinea idea, which was good enough for me. I commissioned my brother P.D. to build some brooder boxes and called the hatchery. A few days later, two boxes of baby guineas—properly called "keets" (as opposed to keats, or Keats, or Byrons or Shelleys for that matter)—were waiting to be picked up at the post office in Fort Wayne.

They were cute. That's how God planned it, I think. He makes guineas cute in the beginning, small and fluffy and helpless looking, so you get attached to them. Then after a couple of weeks the fluff disappears, the cute wears off, and they start getting ugly. You know, kind of like teenagers. At that point you're used to having them around, though, so you're stuck with them. Also like teenagers. He's a tricky one sometimes, that God.

It worked to my advantage, though, because once Mom had the guineas, it was a lot easier to talk her into adding a flock of chicks, which are even cuter. Another call to the hatchery and the next thing you knew, Mom and P.D. were driving to Fort Wayne to pick up the "Meat and Egg Combo"—a collection of cornish rock (meat) birds and several varieties of brown-egg-layers—Mom complaining the entire way that it was just going to be more work for her. Which was absolutely correct.

I got the combo because now, in addition to chicken that tasted like chicken, I wanted eggs that behaved like eggs. You know what I mean. You crack your average supermarket egg into a skillet and the white runs all over the place while the yolk just sits there looking pale and deflated. It's even worse when you poach them. The way they disintegrate, you might as well be making egg drop soup.

A good egg, a real egg, a *fresh* egg, sits up in the skillet and looks at you. The white remains compact. The yolk is bright yellow and plump. The taste is—well, it isn't like chicken. It's like an egg, only more so. It's like the difference between a hothouse tomato and one you've just picked from the garden. Once you've had the real thing, you'll never again be satisfied by those pale imitations in the store, tomatoes or eggs.

Well, Mom and P.D. got the chicks home and got them established, and right away an interesting dynamic occurred. The chicks who would grow up to be laying hens were active and busy, running around doing chicken things—pecking and clucking, and of course, clucking and pecking, and then, when they were done with that, pecking. Also clucking.

The meat birds, on the other hand, followed the imprint of generations of careful breeding designed to turn them into little food-conversion machines. In other words, they parked themselves next to the feeders and remained there, lifting their heads only when someone would come into the chicken house with a new bucket of feed. They were lazy and indolent and living what they thought was the good life, and I suppose it was, considering we're talking about animals with brains the size of a BB. What it was not was the *long* life.

Because of this, my brother avoided giving them names. However, he gleefully assigned names to the laying hens. Right away he began referring to them as Halcyon, Nelta, Ardelle, Mildred, Margaret, and Sharon—Mom's sisters— plus Frances, Connie, Marge, Lucille, Helen, Phyllis, Donna, and Beatrice.

Beatrice didn't keep her name long. Puny, hatched with one eye and a beak that didn't close right, she didn't look like she was going to make it much past adolescence. Since she was a laying hen, and since laying hens have a traditional role to play after they are done laying, one involving a soup pot, some water and vegetables, a few herbs and spices, and some homemade pasta, she was rechristened Noodles.

Chicken and noodles. I adore chicken and noodles. People talk about the breaded tenderloin sandwich, but for my money the official Indiana state food really should be chicken and noodles. You see it everywhere, from the Michigan line to the Ohio River, and it is one of the few things that I have found to be consistently good from one end of the state to the other.

It is, however, most popular in the north. LaGrange County is the heart of what I call Indiana's Noodle Belt. It's an area comprising roughly the northernmost third of the state, where there's a lot of Amish and Mennonite influence on the cuisine, which means you are likely to eat noodles three or four times a week: Chicken and noodles, beef and noodles, and turkey and noodles.

And because this is Indiana, you eat the noodles on a bed of mashed potatoes. It's the Northern Indiana starch load: Noodles, mashed potatoes, and bread and butter on the side. If you're lucky enough to find yourself in South Bend, with its big Polish population, you can get pierogi, which are noodles with the mashed potatoes inside, but usually you just see them the regular way, sitting there in their rich gravy, with the generous hunks of chicken mixed in, resting on fluffy mashed potatoes.

I use chicken and noodles as a way to determine where people are from.

When I'm making a speech, I try to work in a mention of chicken and noodles on a bed of mashed potatoes. If people applaud, I know they're Hoosiers. If their eyebrows go up with alarm, I know I'm dealing with a foreigner. You know, someone from Ohio.

So, anyway, we now had in our flock a chicken named Noodles. No, I didn't name her that. And neither did P.D. That name came from Mom.

I had no idea my mother was so funny.

A mother who can come up with a joke like that certainly does not square with the image of Mom that I carry in my head, the Mom from my kidhood, who always seemed to be on the edge of exasperation, the Mom who set rules and enforced them with an iron hand, the Mom for whom nothing seemed good enough. My report cards, for example. After a pretty good early run, where I came close to being a straight-A student, I lost interest in school and my grades showed it. That meant that every six weeks I would bring home a report card of mostly Bs, with As and Cs here and there—and one horrible day, a day known in the family as Black Friday, an F in chemistry—and every six weeks I would hear my mother pronounce that as far as she was concerned, "a C is the same as an F, a B should be an A, and an A should have been an A the last time."

This was not the kind of Mom who would name a chicken Noodles and then snicker about it.

My brother and I were talking about this recently. Actually, we were discussing our chances of filing a retroactive legal action alleging child abuse. Given today's legal climate, it might just work, although it would probably make for some frosty looks down the table next Thanksgiving.

Our suit, were we to file one, would be over Bactine, or rather, the lack of it. Bactine, at that time, was running commercials on Saturday mornings, right along with the commercials for Sugar-Encrusted Particle Board Flakes and Chocolate Covered Caffeine Bombs, and every commercial made sure to hammer home the fact that when you had a cut or a scape, Bactine did not sting.

To us, this seemed too good to be true, and was. Every other kid on our block had a mom who bought Bactine and used it. Not our Mom. She believed in merthiolate, that red stuff (The Red Badge of Screaming, P.D. calls it) that burned worse than any cut or scrape. You could always tell the Redmond boys in our neighborhood; we were the ones sitting on the curb, blowing desperately at the bright red stains on our knees, while our Mother stood by with the merthiolate bottle telling us to quit being such babies. Easy for her to say. I never saw her putting merthiolate on any of *her* cuts and scrapes.

Then there were the spankings. Other moms used their hands or wooden spoons or hairbrushes, but not our mom. She had a fiberglass rod, three feet long and about the same thickness as the fat end of a fishing pole, that she used to mete out the discipline.

That sucker hurt, but because of its use P.D. and I did acquire an interesting skill: We learned to fly. Mom would grab us by the arm and tell us to hold still so she could spank us. Yeah, like that was going to happen. *Excuse me? You want me to stand here so you can blister my hiney with a three-foot stick that whistles as it slices through the air? No problem. Here, let me take off my pants, make it easier for you.*

So as Mom grabbed us with her right hand, waving the stick with her left, we would begin running counter-clockwise circles around her. As we did this, we would gradually pick up enough speed that our feet would simply leave the floor and there we'd be, flying tight little orbits around Mom while she yelled at us to stand still so she could beat us.

The best she could manage would be a few glancing blows to the calves. Which she would then treat with merthiolate.

OK, that was then. Something happened to Mom over the years. Somewhere along the line she changed. She relaxed. She smiled. She had fun. She lost the fiberglas rod and put a bottle of Bactine in the medicine chest.

She changed from Old Testament Mom, all fire and brimstone and smiting those who transgress, into New Testament Mom, all love and happiness and forgiveness.

What happened to Mom was grandchildren. My sister Vicky kicked it off with her daughters, Amanda and Gillian. Then Amy followed suit with her kids, Deniece and Denephew. By the way, for those who have wondered, those are not their real names. Their real names are Erin and Denephew.

Let me give you some examples of Old Testament Mom vs. New Testament Mom.

Old Testament Mom (OTM): Eat what's on your plate. I'm not running a restaurant here.

New Testament Mom (NTM): Well, if she doesn't like it she doesn't have to eat it.

OTM: You can't have it.

NTM: Well, he wanted it and I just couldn't resist.

OTM: Get out there and do your chores.

NTM: Get out there and tell Uncle P.D. to do his chores.

I knew for sure that we were under the new covenant one Saturday morning when I walked into Mom's kitchen at eight A.M., breakfast time, and saw Deniece and Denephew seated at the kitchen table with big bowls of ice cream. Vanilla.

Ice cream. At eight A.M.

"What are you guys doing?" I asked, incredulous. "Who said you could have ice cream for breakfast?"

"Grandma," they answered.

I went upstairs and found Mom. "Did you tell the kids they could have ice cream for breakfast?"

"They're not hurting anything," she said.

"That's not the point. They're down there at the kitchen table eating ice cream at eight o'clock in the morning. Whatever happened to cereal? Bacon and eggs? Pancakes?"

"They didn't want cereal."

"But Mom, ice cream?"

"Oh, what business is it of yours? So they're having some ice cream. If it makes them happy, so what?"

"Well, then, I guess I'll have some too."

"You'd better not. You're big as a barn already."

Ah ha. So New Testament Mom is just for the little kids. For the rest of us, Old Testament Mom is still very much on the scene.

In fact, when my sister Amy and the kids are at Mom's, it's possible to see Old Testament Mom *and* New Testament Mom at the same time—i.e., the New Testament Mom who loads up the pantry with potato chips is the same person as the Old Testament Mom who chides Amy for letting her kids eat so much junk.

"I never let you kids get away with that," she says. And it's true. She didn't. At dinner we had the three-bite rule, which means that you had to take at least three bites of everything on your plate, whether you liked it or not. To this day, three bites is my limit where liver is concerned.

Meanwhile, Deniece comes to the dinner table and takes one piece of meat and a double helping of Fritos, and if you try to say anything about it, you're told that she gets plenty of good, nutritious food when you're not looking, so butt the hell out and leave the little sweetheart alone.

But we were talking about noodles, weren't we? Which, incidentally, Deniece also will not eat.

The fact that my mother named a handicapped chicken Noodles does indicate, I think, a change for the better in Mom. She is more relaxed these days. She takes things less seriously (obviously). She has a lighthearted quality that was not always present during kidhood (Old Testament Days).

Then again, she was trying to raise four kids to adulthood, four kids with four distinct personalities and four completely different sets of problems, and for much of that time she did it by herself. She had to take things seriously. She couldn't relax. The way she saw it, the second she let down her guard was the second one of us would burn down the house.

Now it's different. Mom has carved out a life for herself that revolves around her farmette, basketball (in season), her cats (Annie, Sophie, and Ike), her bird-watching (we had a big day not long ago when the Redheaded Woodpecker stopped by for a visit), and now, her chickens and guineas.

You call Mom to say hello and you get what I have taken to calling The Rundown:

Mom: Hello.

Mike: Hello. Just calling to ...

Mom: Well, the orioles are building a nest in that hickory tree over by the garage and the heron is over walking around the pond right now. I saw the I.U. game last night and I don't understand why people don't give Coach Davis a break. Last night Annie crawled up into my lap and then Sophie jumped up there and Annie jumped off so Ike chased her upstairs and then in the middle of the night I woke up and there were three cats in bed with me. The guineas wouldn't go back in the chicken house last night until a motorcycle came down the road and then they ran in there like their tails were on fire. Oh, and someone out there laid an egg the size of a baseball. I'm not kidding. It was the biggest egg I've ever seen, but she laid it on the floor and I think one of the guineas stepped on it because it was broken, but it sure was big.

Mike: ... see how you're doing.

Actually, I think the chickens and guineas have been good for Mom, as good as grandkids in a way. For one thing, Deniece and Denephew are teenagers now and inclined to be lippy. You don't get that kind of backtalk from chickens and guineas. Well, come to think of it, you might, but since it isn't in English what difference does it make?

Mom has turned into a chicken aficionado. She pores through the hatchery catalog looking for new breeds to buy, or equipment she thinks we need. She devours books on poultry health and flock management. And she talks of diversifying to include ducks and geese, and maybe a few turkeys. And when she really gets wound up, she thinks about a small herd of goats so she can make goat cheese. That's when I know she is spinning out of control. Lucky for me, I have a one-word solution for that. All I have to say is "Fritzi."

Fritzi was the pet goat of my mother's girlhood. As goats are wont to do, Fritzi liked to climb on things. It was not unusual to see Fritzi on top of the chicken house, or on top of the outhouse, or on top of the garage.

One day, as my mother and her siblings were leaving for school, they saw Fritzi on top of great-grandmother's Reo automobile. When they came home from school that day, Fritzi was nowhere to be found and there was goat for dinner.

Saying "Fritzi" usually stops the cheese idea in its tracks.

My brother, the Chicken Namer, is not much better. He speaks glowingly of certain birds as being "good holding chickens," meaning they will sit still in his lap and let him pet them. More than once I have gone up to Mom's for a weekend only to pull in the driveway and find my brother already there, sitting on the back steps with a little brown hen in his lap. I really wish he'd get a dog.

P.D. has had to do most of the work where the chickens are concerned. Well, that's how he sees it, anyway. I personally think it is a perfectly equitable split of responsibilities, as follows:

P.D.—Repair chicken house and keep it in good shape; build nesting boxes; remove old straw bedding and replace with fresh; keep feed bins full; butcher and clean no-name meat birds; carefully dispose of feathers and non-edible chicken guts.

Mike—Buy chicks and have them sent to Mom's.

Like I said, perfectly equitable.

Besides, all the day-to-day stuff, Mom does. And although she complains, she likes it. I know this because it's like pulling teeth to get her away from them, even for a few days. "I can't leave these chickens," she'll say. Well, yes she can. I have cousins up there who would gladly stop in to feed and water the chickens and collect the eggs. The truth is, she doesn't *want* to leave the chickens. She likes taking care of Halcyon, Nelta, Ardelle, Mildred, Margaret, Sharon, Frances, Connie, Marge, Lucille, Helen, Phyllis, Donna, and Noodles.

Yes, Noodles. The little hen that wasn't going to make it did. In fact, she's one of the more prolific layers in the flock. P.D. and I have a theory about that. We think Noodles overheard us talking about the stewpot and decided that her only chance was to outwork everyone else.

Whatever the reason, I know this: Having the chickens around keeps Mom engaged and active and gives her something to think about besides basketball or her sister Mildred. The rundown used to include a Mildred Report, but I haven't heard one of those in quite a while. Every time I call, though, I hear about something that Noodles did today, which I'll grant you isn't much. She either got on the nest, or got off the nest, and that's about it for Noodles news.

It's kind of weird, I'll admit, but what the heck, Mom's happy. And if Mom's happy, I'm happy. It that was all we got out of the chickens, they'd be worth it. As it turns out, we also get chicken that tastes like chicken and eggs that taste like eggs. Not that the kids would know. They still prefer ice cream for breakfast.

THIRTEEN

If a Picture's Worth a Thousand Words, This Chapter Equals an 8x10, Two 5x7s, and Half a Sheet of Wallets

The boxes were lined up on Mom's dining room table, four across—one for each kid, our names written across the tops in Mom's distinctive, loopy script.

"Take yours home with you," she commanded. "I'm tired of storing this junk for you kids. Clutter up your own house for a change. Throw it away. I don't care. Just get it out of here."

I did as told and took it home, where it remained unopened in a back bedroom. Then I moved. The box came with me and went into another back bedroom, still unopened. I moved again. Same thing. After packing up the dishes and the books, I took the box that said "MIKE" on the top and dragged it, still unopened, to my new address.

Now it sits in a corner of the attic over my garage, where it has remained, un-molested, these four years. I still have not opened it. There's no need. I already know what's in it. Twelve years of humiliation, that's what's in it.

It is a box of school pictures.

School pictures are near the top of all my unpleasant memories of school—and that covers a lot of territory. They're competing with getting stuck in my football pants and having to walk into the science room, past all my laughing classmates, to get Mr. Prisock to help me out of them. Or the time in fourth grade I was accused of horse-laughing when Karen Fitzpatrick sneezed, one of those little cartoon sneezes that sounded like Minnie Mouse, and Mrs. Devane sent me back to the first grade room "until you can learn to act like a big kid." What's worse, it was my brother's classroom and they made me sit at his table. What's even worse than that, he got home before I did that day and ratted me out to Mom.

But those were one-time-only deals. School pictures were an embarrassment that came around every year.

School pictures can be grouped into three categories. There's the Mug Shot, in which the subject stares blankly at the camera and looks as though he or she ought to be holding a board with numbers on it under his or her chin. Actually, now that I think about some of the people I went to school with, the Mug Shot School Picture turned out to be surprisingly prescient.

The second category is the Product Spokesman. These are the "good" school pictures, the ones the school picture companies use in their brochures, the ones where the kids have easy smiles and a self-confident air. They look like they ought to be holding up a pilsener glass in one hand and a pack of cigarettes in the other and saying, "Yep, when I have a rough day staying inside the lines in art class, I like to relax with an ice-cold Falstaff and a delicious, nutritious Kool." Which is a disturbing look for a second-grader.

The third category of school picture is Doofus, and it is into this category that all of my school pictures can be lumped. Twelve years, twelve pictures, twelve examples of Prime American Doofus, mid–twentieth century variety. Twelve years of my classmates looking at my picture at laughing. Twelve years of my parents complaining that all I had to do was sit there and look pleasant and I had somehow screwed it up … *again*.

A Doofus picture may contain any or all of the following:

- Closed eyes.
- One closed eye.
- Crossed eyes.
- Half-smile.
- Half-smile with one closed eye.
- Full smile with crossed eyes.
- Full smile with crossed eyes and missing teeth.
- Hair sticking up in back.
- Hair sticking up in front.
- Hair sticking up all over.
- No hair.

- Crooked necktie.
- Shirt inside-out.
- Shirt backwards.
- Lunchroom spinach on clothes.
- Lunchroom spinach between teeth.
- Lunchroom spinach in hair.
- Foreign object hanging from at least one nostril.
- Humongous zit in middle of forehead, chin, or tip of nose.

Which just about covers all of my school pictures.

School pictures represent another of those battles with parents that kids simply cannot win. One year you do as the photographer asks and give a big cheesy smile and your mom says you ruined the picture by being a smart aleck. The next time you ignore the photographer's entreaties and your mom says you ruined the picture by looking as though the dog died. And in either case, your mother says the pictures are so lousy she's embarrassed to send them to Grandma and it's all your fault.

Or something. I wouldn't want you to think I have issues about this or anything. OK, I do. And I can tell you precisely when it happened: third grade.

We were lined up waiting to get our photos taken, and I was looking spiffy (if I do say so myself). I had the red blazer with the brass buttons and the little yacht club crest on the pocket, I had the clip-on tie with the little locomotives on it. It was my transportation ensemble. And I had my hair combed the way I liked it, with the part in front—the only part of my hair that was actually long enough to need combing—plastered down flat to my head instead of all poofy the way my mother intended.

Up at the head of the line, some volunteer mothers from the P.T.A. were giving kids the once-over before sending them on to the photographer—making sure bangs didn't fall into eyes, removing what remnants of lunch they could find, that sort of thing. And then they would hand out the complimentary pocket comb that I guess was supposed to mollify us—"Well, I hated getting my picture taken, but at least I got a free comb."

I saw, to my horror, that my mom was among the volunteer mothers. I also saw, to my further horror, that she had spied me in line and was making her way toward me.

Without a word she grabbed me out of the line, in front of all my friends, and went to work restoring my hair to its intended style, poofing up the bangs with a rat-tail comb from her purse. Then she grabbed a can of hair spray. You know. The stuff *girls* use.

"NO!" I said.

"Stand still!" she barked. "I need to fix your hair."

"NO! NO HAIR SPRAY! NO HAIR SPRAY!"

"Be quiet and cover your eyes," she said. And she went to work lacquering my hair into place. With hair spray. The stuff *girls* use.

In front of all my friends.

I remember very well the school photo from that day. My bangs are quite poofy, if a little shiny, and the look on my face says nothing more than "future ax murderer." Well, make that "future ax murderer with crooked necktie," which Mom somehow overlooked while she was humiliating me with the Final Net.

It was the practice in those days for the school picture company to prepare a composite photo of the class, thumbnail photos of all the kids and their teachers printed on a four-by-six sheet of paper, and in every one of these composite photos there was always one kid who seemed to be facing the wrong direction. All the other photos would have the kids looking off to the left, but there would always be one kid, and only one, whom the photographer would have looking the other way. And most years of my life, that kid was me. I have no idea why. I do know that it didn't seem to reduce any of the Doofus factor already present in my photos.

And bear in mind, I went to school with a lot of Doofuses. Doofi. Whatever. The point is, you really had to look goofy to stand out in a crowd like that, and I did.

Take the case of my fifth grade class composite picture. A couple of weeks before the pictures arrived, one of my classmates had brought to show and tell his pet chameleon, a lizard of no great talent that I could discern. Mostly he just sat in his little glass box, craned his neck around, and looked at us with his bulging little lizard eyes while his owner, a kid named John, droned on and on about the fascinating world of lizards. Fascinating to him.

OK, fast forward two weeks. School pictures have arrived and are being distributed around the room. Each packet has the standard school picture assortment—one eight by ten for the parents, two five by sevens for the grandparents (this was back in the days when you could take care of your grandparent picture needs with two photos; you didn't need extras to keep things even between grandpa with his third wife and grandma with her live-in boyfriend), twenty or so wallet-sized photos for various friends and relatives, and a composite picture of the class.

Before I had even gotten my packet open, one of my classmates was waving the composite picture in the air and saying, "Mike Redmond looks just like John Gregory's lizard!"

I looked.

He was right.

I was facing the wrong way. My head was tilted up and back, as if I were about to glance over my shoulder. My mouth was drawn tight and my eyes were popping. I looked exactly like John Gregory's lizard, if John Gregory's lizard had been wearing a striped shirt and a crooked black necktie.

Oh, yes, the necktie. That opens up a whole new area of Doofiness (Doofusitude?) known only to kids who changed schools a lot, like army brats or the Redmonds. I went to different schools in fourth, fifth, sixth, seventh, eighth, and tenth grades, and I never knew, going from one school to the other, what the picture protocol might be.

In some schools, the rule was Dress Up For School Pictures. In others, it was Wear Your Normal Clothes For School Pictures. And in other schools, it was a combination: Wear Your Normal Clothes For School Pictures Unless You Are A Member Of The (Basketball, Football, Track, or Audio-Visual) Team, In Which Case, Dress Up. To violate the rule was to declare yourself a Doofus.

For six years I had to guess—was this a dress-up school or a non–dress-up school?—and got it wrong. Every single time.

Picture day would come and I would go to school attired in a crisp shirt and that black necktie (the only one I owned), only to find my T-shirted and blue-jeaned classmates snickering at me. The next year, at a new school, I would show up for pictures wearing whatever I pulled out of the pile in my closet to find my classmates looking down their noses as they brushed the lint from their jackets and adjusted their four-in-hands. The year after that I'd show up in another shirt and that tie again only to find the football team threatening to grind me into paste for violating a sacred school tradition. I couldn't win.

As I entered high school, the wardrobe issue calmed down only to be replaced by a new fight with my parents over my hair.

The issue had been simmering for years. In fact, I can tell you exactly when it began: February 9, 1964, the night the Beatles made their first appearance on the *Ed Sullivan Show*. It was, simply, the coolest thing I had ever seen—guys with guitars and drums, playing catchy music and wearing *long hair*. I can't tell you how great I thought the hair looked.

I can, however, tell you how it stood in stark contrast to my haircut of the time. In fact, I already have. In case you missed it, let's review: It was a crew cut with a little decorative sprig of longer hair in the front, about as far from a Beatle cut as you could get without going for the Yul Brynner look.

The morning after the Beatles appeared on *Ed Sullivan*, I began trying to change my hair—to force the sprig, which stood pretty much straight up (the effects of the hairspray, no doubt) to lie down in some approximation of Beatle bangs.

I also began pestering my mother, who cut our hair, to let me begin growing it down to my ears and collars. My mother refused. "You can't," she said. "Your hair is too bushy for that."

Bushy. I had bushy hair. The way Mom said it, it sounded like a character flaw: "You lie, you cheat, you steal … and you have *BUSHY HAIR*." Oh, the shame.

By the time I reached junior high, I was actually gaining some ground in the hair argument. My bangs began to forget their years of training and inched downward. Occasionally, my hair grazed the tops of my ears, and there were months when it actually fell over my collar, although I had to walk around with my shoulders hunched in order for it to be noticeable. I think most of the back pain I have suffered in my adult life can be traced back to that posture. There are days I can hardly walk upright, and why? Because I wanted long hair when I was thirteen.

Mom knew the cultural winds had changed and long hair was becoming the norm, and so she relented somewhat—although she still reserved the right to give my hair "a quick trim" when school picture time rolled around. Consequently most of the photos from those years show me not as a lizard, but as something along the lines of a freshly-shorn Cheviot sheep. Sheepish, in fact, is the best word to describe the look on my face.

By my junior year of high school the fight was over. My mother no longer had much interest in my hair (other than to remind me, frequently, that it was bushy). She knew enough to know she had lost the fight and that I would be the master of my own tonsorial destiny from then on.

Which gets us to senior pictures.

Senior pictures were an important right of passage at Lakeland High School. You put on your good clothes (no question about it this time) and went to Stopher's Photo Studios in LaGrange sometime in August before your last year of high school. It was your first official act as a senior, and because it took place somewhere other than in front of a backdrop in the cafeteria, your first step toward graduation and independence from the school system that had imprisoned you all those years.

At that time, I was sporting a beard. Well, I called it a beard. It was a strip of whiskers running from one ear to the other, by way of the chin, that I had allowed to grow out of control. Naturally, I was inordinately proud of this chin strap. Strip. Whatever. I considered it proof positive that I was exceptionally cool. Which, of course, I was not.

Lakeland High School had a prohibition against beards on students. I have no idea why. I suppose it was in keeping with that old saying, "If you give them an inch, they'll take a mile," meaning that if you allow boys to grow beards it's only a matter of time before they'll grow ... moustaches. Moustaches were only for teachers. Old lady teachers.

Anyway, I decided to get around the no-beard rule by shaving a one-inch strip on my chin, this converting my beard into a pair of truly ridiculous muttonchop sideburns.

They figured largely in the discussion between my mother and myself the morning I was to go get my senior picture taken, a discussion I now recount in full:

Mom: Go shave off those ridiculous sideburns.
Mike: No.

Mom: All right, but one of these days you are going to look at your senior picture and realize how silly they are.

Mike (*snorting, the condescending nasal blast one expels when dealing with someone who is hopelessly behind the hipness curve, such as a parent*): Oh, please.

Of course, Mom was absolutely right. I looked ridiculous. I looked like I had Brillo pads glued to my cheeks. Not that I realized this right away. Oh, no. It wasn't until years later, when I went home and saw my senior picture on the wall next to Vicky's, P.D.'s, and Amy's, that it struck me that in the most important school picture of all, I had Doofusized myself for all time. Generations of Redmonds yet to be were going to see that picture of great-great-great-great Uncle Mike, with his big dumb sideburns, and say to themselves, "Sheesh. What a *dork.*"

At Mom's, I tend to turn that picture to the wall when I see it. Other places I do not have this luxury. I cannot, for example, go to the houses of all the people who own a copy of the 1972 Lakeland High School yearbook, *The Mirage* (as in "not real"), and cut it out with an X-acto knife, although I'd like to. Neither can I go to the houses of the people who asked for copies of my senior picture and remove it from the picture boxes in their attics, although that would be far easier, as I can only think of about three people who actually asked for them, and I am pretty sure one of those had some sort of voodoo ceremony in mind.

I must contend with the silly thing every five years, when I go back to La-Grange County for a high school class reunion (not including the year my class inexplicably decided to hold its reunion in Goshen, which is in Elkhart County). Invariably someone thinks it would be "cute" to use copies of our senior pictures on our nametags, or someone liberates the big class picture from the high school's Wall Of Honor or Wall Of Graduates or Wall Of Escapees or whatever they call it and brings it to the gathering. And invariably someone will come up to me and say, "What were you thinking with those sideburns?" And the best answer I can come up with—"Well, at least I didn't look like John Gregory's lizard"—means absolutely *nothing*. That was a different school.

So there in the attic sits the box, unopened. I've been thinking about why— why should a grown man be afraid of a few pieces of paper imprinted with images from long ago? I suppose this is something I should take up with a trained mental health professional, but seeing as how it's late at night and the only person I can talk with about it is Cookie, who isn't a person but a dog, I guess I'll have to figure it out on my own.

It could be that those pictures all represent some sort of parental disapproval to me. I can't recall ever bringing one home and hearing Mom say, "Well, that's a nice picture." But that's silly. Whatever issues Mom and I had we worked out long ago, when my therapist gave me a choice between going home and having a heart-to-heart with Mom, or going to the hospital with the soft walls. So I don't think it's parental disapproval.

Maybe it's because I like to think I have acquired a veneer of sophistication as an adult, and to look at those Doofus pictures will somehow prove that I really haven't changed at all. I'm still the same goofball I always was. I just don't have cafeteria spinach in my hair any more.

Or maybe it's just that they're embarrassing.

I think that's the answer. In fact, where the senior picture is concerned, I *know* it is.

Oh, wait. I just remembered. There's one other reason I haven't opened that box:

All my old report cards are in there, too.

FOURTEEN

My Stars!

I am looking at one of my favorite photographs. It shows an old man and woman sitting in side-by-side lawn chairs. She is touching her hair in that "Oh, I must look a fright" way that old ladies do when they see a camera aimed at them. He is leaning forward, forearms resting on his knees, a pipe clasped lightly in his right hand, smiling at the camera as if he were just about to make a joke—which, knowing this old man, he probably was.

They are my Aunt Mildred and Uncle Ceen—great-aunt and great-uncle, actually, my dad's aunt and uncle—and this photo, taken on a sunny day in the back yard of their house in Kendallville, is precisely as I remember them.

Two better people I have never known.

Every time I find myself in Kendallville, Indiana, I make it a point to drive slowly down Dowling Street, past their house. It brings back so many memories, all of them good—we Redmond kids clustered at the front door, ringing the bell; Aunt Mildred coming to the door, opening it, and exclaiming, "My stars!" then coming out onto the porch to hug us and say, "Well, look! Ain't ya growed?"

I remember stepping into the living room to see Uncle Ceen in his chair, watching a baseball game or a boxing match or the news, a metal wastebasket full of half-smoked Prince Albert tobacco between his feet. He never did keep his pipe lit for very long. I remember him grinning and sizing us up: "P.D.'s going to be a middleweight, but it looks like Mike's on the way to heavyweight already."

I remember Uncle Ceen's Aqua-Velva and Lectric Shave bottles, their labels removed, filled with colored water and lined up on the living room windowsill. I remember their shiny aluminum Christmas tree atop the TV, the color wheel slowly rotating to cast it in red light, then yellow, then blue, then green. "Ain't it purty?" Aunt Mildred would say. And yes, we kids thought it was purty, indeed.

I remember the big old clawfoot bathtub where P.D. and I would get scrubbed down after a dusty afternoon at the Noble County fair, the heart-shaped fish pond in the side yard with the huge goldfish swimming lazily about—goldfish that spent their winter months in the basement, in a washtub, where we kids would feed them oatmeal.

I remember the bottle opener on the kitchen wall, just like at the gas station, where you'd put the cap between the jaws, pull down your bottle of 7-Up and hear the satisfying pop, and then the metallic tinkle of a bottle cap dancing on a linoleum floor. Which you then picked up and put in the wastebasket with the pedal that you stepped on to open the lid.

I remember the garden in back, the big vegetable garden bursting with tomatoes and onions and peppers and peas and beans and corn … the only area of the place that was off-limits to unsupervised kids. Uncle Ceen took his gardening *very* seriously.

I remember running through the house at the sound of the passenger train as it approached Kendallville, and then watching through the front window, awestruck, as it zoomed past, just behind the houses across the street.

Mostly, though, I just remember being happy to be there.

Aunt Mildred was my Grandma Redmond's sister, and the two of them struck an interesting balance. The way I always saw it, Grandma could be distant, a little hard to read; Aunt Mildred was warm and open. Grandma was smart—nobody ever beat her at anagrams—while Aunt Mildred tended to rely more on her heart than her brain to guide her through life. Grandma's signature dish was pot roast, which she made every Sunday (and great pot roast it was, too); Aunt Mildred's was butterscotch pie.

And oh, what butterscotch pie it was. Flaky crust, sweet and creamy filling, just the right amount of meringue, browned to perfection. She always had one made, and she always insisted we have a slice almost as soon as we got through the door. We always took her up on it, too. It was fabulous pie. I still have dreams about it.

Because my grandfather Redmond had high-tailed it to Oregon when Dad was two, Uncle Ceen was our grandfather substitute on that side of the family. It fit him well: He smoked a pipe, he knew how to fix things, he told great stories. To our kid minds, that was what grandfathers did.

You pronounced his name "Seen." His full name was Osceen K. May, long "o" on the first name, which I believe was a version of the ancient Irish name Ossian, as in Ossian the bard, Ossian who left Ireland for the land of Tir Na N-og.

Or maybe his parents just made it up, because I have never met another Osceen and I don't think I'm likely to.

Whatever the origin, I always thought it was a great name because of the initials. Uncle Ceen went by his initials for correspondence, you see, so all the magazines that came to his house were sent to "O.K. May." O.K. May. I thought that was snappy.

Uncle Ceen was a self-made man—not in the millionaire sense, but in another and I think more meaningful way. Orphaned while still a boy, he went to work at an age when most of us are still learning how to ride our two-wheelers.

I'm not sure of *all* the work he did. I know he was a lineman for a while. He used to like to show me a picture of himself standing atop a utility pole, arms outstretched. He owned a service station in Kendallville. He worked at McCray, the refrigerator company, and when he retired from there went to work for Kraft at the candy factory.

The Kraft job paid a fringe benefit we kids enjoyed. Every month after he retired (the second time), the company would send a honking big box of those little cellophane-wrapped caramel cubes to Aunt Mildred and Uncle Ceen. They always had a big bowl of them on the dining room table, and we kids were invited to help ourselves. When it was empty there were always more to fill it back up again. And when it was time to go home, Aunt Mildred always told us to fill our pockets before we left.

She was just that way. With the exception of the garden, I cannot recall a single instance of Aunt Mildred ever saying no to a kid. This, of course, stood in sharp contrast to our parents, for whom no was the customary answer to … well, just about everything.

One of the big attractions at Aunt Mildred and Uncle Ceen's house was a set of drums in one of the upstairs bedrooms. These belonged to my Dad's cousin Jim, their son, but like a fool he left them behind when he went into the service, and then to college, and then to his grownup life. Well, it seemed foolish to P.D. and me, anyway. Anybody who had drums and didn't take them everywhere he went was making a serious mistake, in our book.

We would ask our mother if she thought it would be all right for us to go upstairs and play the drums. Mom, of course, always said no.

Then we would ask Aunt Mildred. "Land sakes, yes," she would say. "Go right ahead."

We'd dash up the stairs and start whaling away. P.D. always went for the snare but I preferred the deeper sound of the tom-toms. I was a faithful watcher of Bomba the Jungle Boy movies on Saturday afternoons. Tom-toms figured largely in Bomba the Jungle Boy movies. Tribe down the river up to no good? You could tell by the tom-toms. Need to send a message to the constabulary? Grab a drum and start pounding. Elephants on the stampede? Quick, get me a drum so I can turn this herd.

So we would be thumping and crashing away, P.D. on the snare, me on the herd-turner, and Mom would appear in the doorway. "I thought I told you no," she would say.

"Aunt Mildred said we could," we would chorus, knowing that Aunt Mildred outranked Mom in this case and we had trumped Mom's ace. Then we would go back to our drum duet, crashing and banging and letting all of Aunt Mildred's neighbors know that the Redmond kids were visiting again.

Now, when you are a little kid and you have a great-aunt and great-uncle who have unlimited caramels, butterscotch pie, and drums in their house, you want to go there all the time. The interesting thing about Aunt Mildred and Uncle Ceen was we all wanted to keep visiting as we got older. You know how it is with teenagers—they'd rather drink lye than spend an afternoon with elderly relatives. But it was not that way with Aunt Mildred and Uncle Ceen.

P.D. and I were getting our teeth straightened by an orthodontist in Kendallville. I would drive us down there for our adjustments and as soon as we were done, we'd head on over to Dowling Street and ring the bell. "My stars!" Aunt Mildred would say when she saw us. "Ain't ya growed?" We might have only been there a week before, but as far as Aunt Mildred was concerned, we had always growed.

Uncle Ceen would be there, in his chair, watching a ball game, drinking a beer (Drewrey's, at first, and later Genesee). Sometimes Aunt Mildred would have a beer, too. They even gave me one when I turned eighteen. I loved that.

Me, my great-uncle, and my great-aunt sitting in the living room, sipping our beers and watching the World Series.

Uncle Ceen followed politics closely, and he had opinions about everything that was going on in Washington. What was cool was that he expected you to have an opinion, too. He didn't care if you were only eighteen years old and not completely sure which end was up. It didn't even matter so much what your opinion was—if it was opposite Uncle Ceen's, he enjoyed the debate. What mattered was that you thought about something and made up your mind about what you believed about it. That's what he was trying to teach us: To use our minds.

And he gave me some advice I have never forgotten:

"Don't be too liberal," he would say. "If you're too liberal, no one will trust you. And don't be too conservative. If you're too conservative, no will like you. And for God's sake, don't ever lose your sense of humor. You won't be able to make it without a sense of humor."

I still miss them. I look at this picture of them and I miss them terribly. I want them to see me now, as an adult, using my mind with, I hope, my sense of humor intact. I want them to see that I can make a butterscotch pie (although it's not nearly as good as Aunt Mildred's). I want them to see that the warmth and love they gave all of us kids still lives within us.

I want them to see that I've growed, and they were a big part of it.

FIFTEEN

Deniece and Denephew

I am, on my mother's side, a McKenzie. Chances are this means nothing to you, but in LaGrange County, the little place in Northern Indiana that I call home, it speaks volumes. The McKenzies are an old family in LaGrange County, well-known and respected despite everything my cousins and I have done to turn the tide of popular opinion. At least, that's the way our parents put it.

McKenzies have reputations for being hard workers (except for me) and for being smart (no comment), and there *is* some truth to it. We have a bunch of high achievers in the family, achievers like my Uncle Bruce, the professor at Purdue, or Uncle John, who went through college with straight As, or Uncle Verl, who was a big-time businessman.

My generation has had its achievers, too, but we also have in us a strong streak of what I call the knucklehead factor. According to our parents, this has only begun to show up in our generation of the family. Ask any of my cousins. Each one of us has heard Standard McKenzie Parent Speech Number 614, "We *never* acted like that when we were children."

The knucklehead factor shows up in me—heck, I've made a career out of writing about it.

It has shown up in my cousin Eldon, whose childhood misadventures are the stuff of family legend. Eldon was the one who threw the firecracker into the charcoal grill just as my Mom was about to start cooking hamburgers. Eldon was the one who shot me with a BB gun and then tried to get out of it by saying, "I didn't know it was loaded." Eldon was the one who climbed a tree at Grandpa's and then leaned back to relax on a limb, smiling smugly, at which point the limb promptly gave way. Watching Eldon fall out of that tree was like watching a cartoon. He'd hit a limb and it would crack, sending him down to the next limb, which would crack, sending him down to the next limb, which would crack, and so on until he finally landed on the lawn with a hollow thump. Daffy Duck couldn't have done it better.

There was my cousin Grant, who while taking P.D. and me for a ride on his motorbike thought it would be fun to scare up the bees in Uncle John's hives. He zoomed close and gunned the engine as P.D. and I shrieked with protest. Then he got stung, repeatedly, while P.D. and I escaped unharmed, which leads me to believe he had done this before and the bees were sick and tired of it.

There was my cousin Nate, who went riding through Sturgis on a motorcycle, and was just congratulating himself on how cool he looked, when he turned his head to yell at a girl he knew … and ran right into the back of a car. Might even have been a cop car.

Then there's my cousin John, my kidhood hunting partner. We were out with BB guns one day, shooting at and missing sparrows. The sparrows had gotten tired of us shooting at them and flown out of range, so John leveled his BB gun and aimed it toward a large boar Uncle Maurice was keeping in a pen next to the barn.

"Watch this," he said, squeezing the trigger. The BB flew out of the barrel and hit the boar squarely in the … in the … well, in the things that make him a boar and not a sow, if you get my drift. The ol' moneymakers. His, um, hoo-hoos.

The hog grunted and shuddered and did what any male would do under those circumstances, which is pull them up and, presumably, out of the line of fire.

"My turn," I said, as I took aim and squeezed off a shot of my own. Same thing—grunt, shudder, pull.

"OK, me again," said John.

At that point, John's older brother Tom—three years John's senior—walked up and began reading us the riot act as only older brothers can.

"Stop that right now!" he said. "You know better than to shoot a boar in the nuts!"

"Oh, come on," said John. "They're only BBs."

Tom didn't hesitate a second.

"Oh, sure," he said, "they're BBs today, but what if one day you're out here with a .22, only you forget that it's a .22 and you think it's just a BB gun, and you shoot him in the nuts with a .22? Then what?"

Well, we had to admit he had us there. Tom had trapped us in the snare of logic. And since that day, I have never, ever thought I had a BB gun in my hand when I was carrying a .22. Thanks, Tom. The world may never know how many boars you saved.

OK, so you can see that the knucklehead factor was alive and well in my generation of the family.

Well, I am here to tell you that it has been passed along. We're all parents and grandparents now, and I can assure you that there are lots of little McKenzie family knuckleheads running around doing the same kind of stupid stuff we used to do. And, in some cases, improving on it. My sister's kids, Deniece and Denephew, come to mind.

I am thinking of the time my sister and her family lived in Hawaii, owing to my brother-in-law John's assignment to Schofield Barracks, the army installation on Oahu.

I don't know if you're aware of this, but there's a federal statute that says if you have family members living in Hawaii, you are required by law to go visit them. Really, it was out of my hands. For me to get on that plane and fly from snowy Indiana out to the land of palm trees and sunshine, pineapple and hula dancers, warm breezes, and roaring surf—well, I was just being a good citizen. Never let it be said that I disobeyed the law of the land. Unless you count speeding, underage drinking, and theft of road signs.

So, at any rate, I went off to our fiftieth state to see the palm trees, sunshine, pineapple, hula dancers, and also my sister and her kids, then about ages six (Deniece) and five (Denephew).

Now, the law says you have to visit your family in Hawaii but it doesn't say you have to stay with them. Therefore, while they remained ensconced at Schofield Barracks, where the average size of a noncommissioned officer's living room is roughly equal to the place in your kitchen where you keep the canned goods and extra paper towels, I billeted myself at the Sheraton Moana Surfrider, which I would recommend highly even though they're not giving me a nickel for plugging it in this book.

It's one of the two "old" hotels on Waikiki, the other being the Royal Hawaiian. The Royal Hawaiian is the one also known as the pink palace, because it is the exact same color as Pepto-Bismol. The Moana, on the other hand, is white, with a broad veranda. Which, now that I think about it, reminds me of several of my relatives, who also are white, with broad verandas.

The Moana is known for the presence of a banyan tree in its courtyard. Under this tree, legend has it, Robert Louis Stevenson sat and wrote … something. A letter home, I think. Maybe some postcards. Or a laundry list. At any rate, that really sold me on the hotel. I thought maybe if I sat under that same banyan tree, some of that Robert Louis Stevenson literary mojo might rub off on me. As you can see, it didn't happen.

The Moana is also known for a spectacular Sunday breakfast brunch, and it was here that I first became aware that the knucklehead factor had been passed along to a new generation.

I had decided that I would treat my family to brunch. It was my way of showing them that I love them, my way of thanking my sister for showing me around Hawaii, my way to play Head Of The Family. I wanted to be able to sit at the head of a big table with all my family arrayed around me, plates full, faces beaming, and know that life was rich and good.

So along came Sunday morning, and brunch. We met in the hotel's open, airy lobby, and ambled pleasantly toward the dining room—a stately ballroom, actually, with polished floors and beautiful furnishings and a gorgeous view of the beach. Just as we passed the concierge desk, I saw the sign:

Sunday Brunch

$40 per person

Let's see. There was me. My girlfriend, Judith. My sister. Her neighbor. The kids. Her neighbor's kids. Eight people at $40 a head. No, this was not one of those kids-eat-free deals. It was $40 a head, period.

After a moment of waffling (brunch, waffling, get it?), I decided, What the hell? You only go around once. This was why God invented American Express gold cards, right? In we went.

Arrayed around the room was one of the most spectacular displays of food I have ever seen outside of a family reunion: Fresh fruit by the ton, glistening with sweet juice; pastries of all shapes, arrayed in great mountains; six or seven kinds of grilled meats; eggs cooked to order; waffles made as you waited; cold cuts and cheeses; breads of all colors and descriptions; acres and acres of salads; and on one long table, mountains of desserts, each gooier and creamer than the one before it.

And that was just the American side. This being Hawaii, there was a complete Japanese buffet as well. I wandered over thinking I might try something from the Japanese side, just for kicks, but I pretty quickly decided against it. Miso soup is great, but I have a hard time thinking of it as the breakfast of champions.

Back over to the American side I went, where I loaded up on more familiar fare—eggs, sausages, potatoes, fruit, toast—the kind of stuff that made the Japanese wonder how we could eat such crap—and had just sat down when Deniece came up and plopped down in the chair beside me.

On her plate were two pieces of sausage and a waffle.

Let's do the math, shall we? At $40 a head, Deniece had a $13.33 waffle and $26.66 worth of sausage.

"Oh no you don't," I said. "I am not paying $40 for a waffle the size of a coaster and two measly little pieces of sausage. You get back over there and get something else."

"But I don't like anything else," she whined.

"Sure you do," I said, knowing full well that she was telling the truth. Deniece was—is—the world's pickiest eater. She really *could* walk into a banquet hall full of food and not find anything she liked. We're still marveling over that day in 1992 when Deniece voluntarily ate a vegetable.

Well, she didn't believe me when I told her she liked lots of things on the buffet line.

"No I don't," she said, slumping down in her chair and kicking her feet.

"Yes you do," I said.

"*No I Don't!*" she yelled. All around the room, heads swiveled to see who was causing the ruckus.

Judith jumped in.

"Why don't we go see if there's something else you might just want to try," she said, leading Deniece gently toward the desserts. A few minutes later, they were back with a bowl of chocolate mousse, which Deniece did not touch.

Now, Denephew has never been as quite as fussy about food as Deniece. At various family dinners over the year, he has—after some cajoling—eaten goose, lamb, and squirrel, which his sister would not touch under threat of starvation. Although now that I think about it, "eaten" may be too strong a word. I don't think you can say you've "eaten" something if all you've really done is pop a tiny little sliver of something into your mouth and then swallow it without chewing. Or tasting. Still, that hasn't stopped him from going home and bragging to his friends about all the exotic food he eats up at Grandma's.

That morning in Hawaii, however, he gave his sister a run for the money when he noticed that the scrambled eggs were not dry, the way he likes them, but moist and creamy.

"Uncle Mike," he said, making a face, "it's not fine." At the time, "not fine" was about the worst something could be in Denephew's world.

So off the plate and onto the tablecloth went the eggs, along with the sausage that had touched them, the toast that had touched the sausage, and the fruit that had touched the toast.

Meanwhile, Deniece was staring sullenly at her chocolate mousse.

"Are you going to eat that?" I asked. Stupid question.

"No," she said.

"I'll eat it!" Denephew chimed in.

"OK," said Deniece, her face brightening. She slid the bowl over to Denephew and hopped down from the table.

About twenty minutes later, Judith noticed that Deniece had not returned to the table and was, in fact, nowhere to be seen.

"Of course not," said Amy, with not the slightest trace of concern on her face. "Didn't you see the ladies' room? It has full-length mirrors. She's in there putting on a show."

Judith went into the ladies' room, and sure enough, there was Deniece, oblivious to the presence of any other human beings, about halfway through this week's broadcast of *The Deniece Show*, pretending to hold a microphone and introducing her very special guest star, a close personal friend, a warm and wonderful human being and a fabulous talent … herself.

Meanwhile, back at the table, Denephew had polished off Deniece's mousse and about two other bowls besides. He had just laid down his spoon when all that high-octane sugar and chocolate kicked in. The next thing we knew, he was zooming around the room, caroming off tables, running up the walls, swinging from the chandeliers. The stately ballroom of the Moana, our corner of it, anyway, was beginning to resemble the primate house at the Lincoln Park Zoo, or an old Johnny Weissmuller movie: *Tarzan Goes to Brunch*.

Amy gathered up Denise and Denephew—or, as we were now calling him,

Cheetah—and took off for the swimming pool to burn off some of that extra energy, while Judith and I got ready for the evening's festivities: A luau.

We had no choice in the matter. See, there's another law at work here, a Hawaii state law, which says that visitors from the mainland cannot leave the island unless they attend at least one (1) luau. When you land, they hand you a luau card and if it hasn't been stamped by the time you return to the airport, they won't let you get on the plane. Many a tourist has missed his flight home because he had to go attend an emergency, last-minute luau at one of those cocktail lounges near the airport.

Amy had arranged for us to attend the official U.S. Army luau. Yes, there really was such a thing. And it was just what you'd expect from a government luau: everything supplied by the lowest bidder.

The food, for instance. At the center of every luau is roast pork. Now, I am a Hoosier boy, and I love my pork, but U.S. Army roast pork is another beast entirely. I am pretty sure this particular roast pork was leftover from World War II. I suspect it had been sitting, in giant pig-shaped cans, in an ammo dump somewhere near Schofield since about 1944, and it tasted like it. Let's put it this way: Once I ate U.S.Army luau pork, I was no longer squeamish about Spam.

Then there's the lomi lomi salmon, or, as we call it on the mainland, lox. Unfortunately, there is no such thing as a luau bagel, or it might have gone down a little easier.

Then comes poi. The less said about poi the better. Remember that kid in first grade who ate the library paste? Poi eater.

Add to that the entertainment—an egregiously cheesy lounge act—and you can see why, when Amy announced to the kids that we were all going to a luau, they hid under their beds.

"I'll tell you what," Amy said. "If you're awake on the way home from the luau, maybe we can stop at McDonald's."

At this, the kids poked their heads out from under the beds. Covered with dust bunnies, an old sock hanging from Denephew's hair, they asked their mom: "Really? McDonald's?"

"Maybe," said Amy. "If you're awake."

Amy, as you have no doubt noticed, was stacking the deck. She mentioned McDonald's as a come-on because every American child is born wanting to go to McDonald's. It's true. They come out of the womb asking for French fries.

But she also used two words that mothers frequently employ when they're trying to gain the upper hand—"If" and "Maybe." Not that the kids heard them. The kids heard nothing except the word "McDonald's." Ah, McDonald's. Home of the classic kid meal, the Happy Meal: A burger that will only have three bites taken from it, a bag of fries that will wind up jammed into the seat cushions, a drink that will spill all over the carpet, and a toy that will break before you get out of the parking lot. No wonder kids love it so much.

Now, Amy knew a few things the kids didn't, or at least had forgotten in their McDonald's mania: Number one, that the luau wouldn't be over until well past their bedtime, meaning they would be exhausted; Number two, it was a long and boring drive home; and Number three, even in the middle of a bright, sunny day the kids could hardly go four blocks in the car without falling asleep. There was no way those kids were going to stay awake all the way home. Amy was pretty sure she had "iffed" and "maybed" the kids into going to a luau against their wishes, and that she wouldn't have to go to McDonald's, either.

The luau ended well after ten P.M. We hauled the kids, already half-asleep, to the car and began the drive up from Waikiki to Schofield. Sure enough, the kids were zonked out by the second stop light and remained that way right up until we parked the car.

That is when Denephew noticed we were in the driveway, not the drive-through, and went into a kid meltdown that even rivaled those legendary tantrums thrown by his Uncle P.D.

"You said we could go to McDonald's! You said we could go to McDonald's! You said we could go to McDonald's!" he wailed, kicking his feet and grabbing the seat belt, clinging to it like a drowning sailor going for a life saver, as Amy tried to remove him from the car.

"I said if you were awake, maybe we could go to McDonald's," Amy replied coolly.

"You said we could go to McDonald's! You said we could go to McDonald's!" Now he was lying in the driveway. Deniece, showing some smarts for a change, stayed out of it. She just stood there and watched, wide-eyed, as her brother convulsed and screamed. "You said we could go to McDonald's! You said we could go to McDonald's!"

Then he pulled that trick that kids do where they increase their body weight by factors of hundreds. In an instant, Denephew went from thirty-five pounds soaking wet into a little inert mass that tipped the scales somewhere in the ton-and-a-half range. I know, because I was the one charged with getting him into the house, and it took a winch, a team of mules, two jeeps, and a crowbar just to get him to the living room, where he lay on the floor and continued to shriek: "You said we could go to McDonald's! You said we could go to McDonald's!"

Lights were coming on all over the post. It was only a matter of time before somebody called the MPs to report a child being held against his will somewhere in the non-com housing. And Amy had had enough.

"Listen to me!" she hissed. "I said if you were awake, maybe we could go to McDonald's. *If. Maybe.* You weren't awake. You were asleep."

Denephew stopped screaming. He raised his head, fixed his mother with a cold stare, and said:

"My eyes are open. Are you blind?"

It was three years before that kid saw the inside of a McDonald's again.

But it was a valuable lesson for me. Thanks to Denephew, I learned beyond a shadow of doubt that the knucklehead factor had, indeed, been passed along to a new generation of McKenzies. In fact, it might even been stronger in that generation than it was in mine, considering the way that kid backtalked his mother. We *never* did that when *we* were kids.

SIXTEEN

Making Change

OK, well, it is sort of a book about change. I mean, the people and events I chose to write about all changed me somehow, in most ways for the better, I hope. Boy, do I hope. I mean, I really, really hope.

See, as I look back at the last fifty years, I don't always like what I see. I see arrogance and smugness and stubbornness, all of which are, of course, public faces of insecurity. I see an annoying know-it-all refusing to consider that someone else might have the right idea once in a while. I see a lot of decisions that, on reflection, were exactly the wrong thing to do. I see someone who always, always, had a lot of growing up to do.

But enough about my brother.

(Just kidding, P.D. Except about the stubbornness.)

I see that my whole life has been about change. That is life. Change is the constant in human existence. How we adapt to it, how we make use of it, how we grow from it—that's what separates a good life from one that didn't reach its potential. Having heard all my life about how I wasn't reaching my potential (and how the next bad thing I did was going to go on my Permanent Record), I think it's time to start.

The nice thing is you get another chance to make it better every time the sun comes up.

The people and places and events I have written about did change me, some in large ways and some in small ways, but they're not the whole story, not by a long shot. There are lots of other people and places and events I had to leave out, or chose to leave out. Some aren't pleasant. Some I just couldn't make funny. And some are still in the process of doing whatever it is they're supposed to do, like my friend Papaw, who came into my life for one reason and, to my everlasting gratitude, stayed there for another. I told him I'd mention him in the book. Hey there, Papaw. By the way, Papaw's writing a book of his own. I can't wait to read it. He's calling it *Don't Judge a Book by Its Cover* and all I can tell you is that in Papaw's case, that is very good advice.

The last few years of my life have been the time of the concentrated period of change, at a time when you'd think things would start to slow down. Typical me. When everyone else is getting off the gas, I start cracking the throttle.

And, in fact, the greatest change of my life, the most wonderful thing that ever happened to me, happened only about two years ago. I can't tell you what it was, though. You'll just have to read about it in the next book. Which I have to start working on right away.

Mike Redmond
Indianapolis, Indiana